FROM UNDERDOG TO BULLDOG

—FROM UNDERDOG— —TO BULLDOG—

MY JOURNEY AS A COLLEGE FOOTBALL WALK-ON

CANDLER COOK

LIONCREST
PUBLISHING

FROM UNDERDOG TO BULLDOG
My Journey as a College Football Walk-On

ISBN 978-1-5445-1381-2 *Hardcover*
     978-1-5445-1380-5 *Paperback*
     978-1-5445-1379-9 *Ebook*

To my parents, Gregg and Penni, and my sisters, Carsen, Courtlyn, and Cayden. You're always there for me, and you all played an important role in my journey.

CONTENTS

FOREWORD

At the University of Georgia, commitment and dependability are two qualities that are expected of the faculty, students, and fans. Commitment to the G takes passion, dedication, and heart. Candler Cook embodies all of these qualities.

Candler is an outstanding man who cannot be knocked down. When the world says he can't, he says, "I can." When the world tells him to stay down, he stands up. When the Georgia football team tells him no—not once, but twice—he trains, he learns, and he grows, until they can only say yes. Candler's ability to fight and keep pushing forward is what made him destined for success.

Candler did not believe in limitations. He did not believe anyone had control over what he could accomplish. He had a hard and long road to the football field. Some days involved tough lessons and moments of doubt. However, he continued to believe in himself despite the obstacles he faced. Candler was resilient in pursuing his dream. His constant determination and accountability to others was his fuel for success. Furthermore, this resilience and determination are what ultimately led to him walking out on the field of Sanford Stadium and hearing thousands of people cheer on his accomplishment.

Candler was always the first person to say thank-you in any situation. He exemplified a servant's heart in the fact he was always willing to do what was necessary while maintaining a positive attitude. He was the type of young man who was willing to go the extra mile in every aspect of his life. His love for Georgia and his family is unlike any other.

I was truly humbled and, honestly, floored when Candler reached out to me about this book. I have no doubt that the people who choose to read his story will be just as impacted by him as I was. Through knowing Candler, I learned about passion, resilience, and dedication. I was reminded of these qualities and how crucial they are to the way we carry ourselves throughout life.

Candler's book may be about the 1,543 days between when he first asked to try out for the team and the day he played against New Mexico State his senior year, but the qualities and values he exemplified during those days transcend time. I hope the readers of this book enjoy learning from Candler as much as I did.

—Rodney Garner, associate head football coach, Auburn University, and former assistant head football coach, University of Georgia

INTRODUCTION

Georgia trailed 28-7 at the start of the third quarter. My dad and I sat side by side on the sofa, glued to the TV. This wasn't just any game. This was Georgia versus Auburn—a road game against our oldest rival—and we were losing by twenty-one points.

"Dinner's ready," Mom called from the kitchen.

Dad and I reluctantly left our spot on the couch and joined my mom and sisters at the dining room table. Anytime we heard cheering, Dad and I ran back into the living room to see what we had missed. We ran back and forth so often that our food got cold, and we finally left most of it uneaten.

With less than forty seconds left in the game, Georgia had closed the lead to 28-21, and the offense was driving down the field. Then Auburn sacked the quarterback with seconds remaining. Thinking the game was over, the Auburn defense began celebrating and one of the players picked up the ball and started running away with it. The referee blew his whistle: there was still time on the clock; the game was not over. The ref brought the ball back to the line of scrimmage, and on the next down, Georgia spiked the ball with a second left to set up one last play.

Dad and I were on the edge of the sofa, watching the TV and listening to Georgia's iconic announcer, Larry Munson, on the radio. After Georgia broke from the huddle, Munson said, "We come up to the line. The stadium rocks and rolls. There's no way we do it with one second. Snap, we pick up the blitz, and Bobo throws that thing in the end zone and...YES! Touchdown! Touchdown on the goal line!" My dad and I leaped up and cheered like we had just won the game. Georgia, the underdog in this contest, had just sent the game into the first overtime in SEC history.

In overtime, each team scored a touchdown, forcing a second overtime. Georgia and Auburn both scored again, forcing overtime number three.

At this point, the game had gone well over the usual three-and-a-half-hour mark, and it was definitely past my bedtime. I was seven, and I usually didn't get to watch late games for this very reason. "Isn't it time for bed?" my mom asked, poking her head into the living room.

"It is, but the game's in overtime!" my dad replied. He knew how special this game was. We were watching history. The one hundredth meeting between these rivals had turned into one long and crazy game.

In the third overtime, both teams scored. The game was now tied at 49–49. In the fourth overtime, Georgia scored first. Then the defense came out and shut down Auburn three plays in a row. It all came down to the next play. On the fourth down, Auburn ran the ball, but Georgia again made the stop. My dad and I jumped off the sofa, screaming and high-fiving. The marathon was finally over; we won!

After the game I went straight to bed, but not to sleep. I was too excited. Highlights from the game danced through my head. I kept replaying the touchdown pass at the end of regulation and the back-and-forth scoring throughout the four overtimes. I thought about the amazing comeback from twenty-one points down. I loved how the team never gave up, even when the odds were against them. They just kept pushing and pushing, and finally came out on top.

Before that game, I enjoyed watching football with my

dad. It was something we did every week in the fall. I looked up to the players and thought it would be great to play football at Georgia. After that game, I *knew* I wanted to be on that field someday. I wanted to be a Georgia football player. Now I just had to figure out how to get there.

Even if you live, eat, and breathe college football, you may not know what really goes on behind the scenes. This book will give you an insider's look into the world of off-season workouts, mat drills, practices, and team traditions. I'll share my walk-on experience and the ridiculous measures I took both on and off the field to make the team and become a Georgia Bulldog.

This book is also for anyone with a seemingly impossible goal. I was just an average guy. I wasn't a standout on my high school football team; in fact, I wasn't even a starter. I was a fourth-string linebacker and had recorded one tackle in my entire high school career. Yet I successfully tried out for and walked on to one of the top football programs in the country. Each chapter details a step in my process and ends with tips you can apply to your own seemingly impossible goal.

When I was seven years old and decided I wanted to be a Bulldog, I hadn't even played on a football team yet.

After I started playing, my determination only grew. Like Georgia in that four-overtime win, I kept pushing and pushing until my dream became a reality. I went from underdog to Bulldog—and so can you.

CHAPTER 1

THE DREAM GROWS

There's two times of year for me: football season, and waiting for football season.

—DARIUS RUCKER

When I was growing up, my dad took me to two or three home games each football season. We woke up early, dressed in red and black Georgia gear, and made the hour-and-fifteen-minute drive from Atlanta to Athens. On the road we listened to the pregame show to catch the breakdown of the matchup, an analysis of our opponent's strengths and weaknesses, and the injury reports—all the details dedicated fans like us wanted.

The excitement I felt driving into Athens on game day can only be compared to the excitement I felt each Christmas morning. No matter how early we arrived, people were already tailgating on Milledge Avenue, a street that leads into the Georgia campus. Fans parked their cars off the main street and then set up canopies, chairs, and barbecues on the grass in front of houses and local businesses. People spent the hours before kickoff watching TV, grilling out, tossing a football, and talking about the upcoming game. It was an all-day event.

When we turned from Milledge Avenue onto Baxter Street, we caught our first glimpse of Sanford Stadium. We parked and moved with the crowd toward the west end, where the stands are lower than the rest and provide a view into the stadium from a block away. As we walked over the bridge overlooking the west end zone, the whole field came into view.

My dad and I always arrived three to four hours before kickoff. Sometimes we tailgated with his friends, and sometimes the two of us hung out and got something to eat. Either way, we always made our way to the stadium about two hours before game time to attend the Dawg Walk. Almost every college program has their version of this event: the team takes a bus to the stadium, and fans line up to greet the players as they exit, holding banners and giving high fives. The Georgia band plays the fight song while majorettes and cheerleaders perform. The Dawg Walk is the first big event of each game day, and ten thousand fans are usually on hand to welcome the players into the stadium.

After the Dawg Walk, we found our seats. Dad had season tickets in the southeast corner of the lower level, near the end zone. As we watched warm-ups and other pre-game rituals, my anticipation grew. About ten minutes before kickoff, one single trumpeter stood in the southwest corner of the upper deck and played the first few notes of "Battle Hymn of the Bulldog Nation." Then the trumpeter stopped, and the rest of the song played over a loudspeaker while the big screen showed highlights of Georgia players past and present.

Once the game started, Dad and I talked about what was happening on the field. We knew the players' names, jersey numbers, and stats. We knew who had just been recruited out of high school. I made a point of learning the jersey numbers of the new freshmen before the season started, and each week I read up on the team we were facing. If I didn't understand a certain play, I asked Dad to explain. When Georgia scored, we were out of our seats, cheering and high-fiving.

On the drive home after a win, we talked about the game and listened to the postgame show to hear the stats and get the commentators' take on the game. If Georgia lost, however, we didn't talk much, and we usually changed the radio to music instead of the commentary. Either way, we stopped at John's Barbecue on the way home, a family-owned barbecue place in Hoschton, Georgia. I ordered the same thing every time: a pulled-pork sandwich, french fries, and hush puppies. Good ole Southern food.

Game days with my dad continued through high school. The more I watched, the more firmly entrenched my goal of playing at Georgia became.

YOUTH LEAGUE

In the fall of 1999, when I was ten years old, my parents signed me up for my first football team. At the tryout, the coaches put everyone through different drills to look at skill level and experience, and later they conducted a draft to divide us into teams. The teams were named after college football programs, and Georgia was one of them.

After the tryout, I talked to my dad about what I saw as a very serious situation: "Dad, what if I'm not picked to play for Georgia?"

"Well, then you'll play for another team," he replied.

I shuddered at the thought. I could not imagine wearing a football jersey with any name but Georgia. To this day, I don't know if my dad put in a special request, but I was indeed picked to play for Georgia.

About six months after I started playing, my dad invited

me to go with him on a special trip to the University of Georgia. He worked for Georgia Power, and some of the company's employees were invited to tour the football facilities and watch a spring practice.

I was so excited. I proudly wore my youth league Georgia football jersey. We met at my dad's office in Atlanta and boarded a chartered bus for the trip. During the drive, we all played a Georgia football trivia game, and my dad and I knew more than our fair share of the answers.

When we arrived, one of the coaches, Joe Tereshinski Jr., went over the schedule for the day. At the time, Coach Tereshinski worked in football operations as a video coordinator. After he briefed our group and dismissed us, my dad approached Coach Tereshinski, told him I played offensive line, and asked if he had any pointers. Coach showed me proper pass- and run-blocking techniques and talked about the importance of hand position while blocking. Little did I know that Coach T, as I would later know him, would figure prominently in my future quest to become a Georgia Bulldog.

During our visit, we saw the athletic director's office and the trophy room where they kept the 1980 national championship trophy, the Heisman trophies, and jerseys that had been retired. As I looked around, I kept thinking, *Man, I really want to do this!*

Our next stop: the practice field. We watched the end of a spring practice, and then some of the players came over to talk with us. I was blown away by being so close to the guys I idolized. I even got my picture taken with a few, including future NFL player Will Witherspoon and Georgia's quarterback at the time, Quincy Carter. I also got my picture taken with the head coach, Jim Donnan. I went home that night with a huge smile on my face. I couldn't believe I had just met the players and coaches I spent Saturdays watching on TV.

Trip to the University of Georgia with my dad's company, March 2000. Standing next to me is Will Witherspoon, and kneeling is Charles Grant.

MIDDLE SCHOOL

In seventh grade, I started playing football for my school. Our quarterback was the son of Doug Williams, a Super Bowl MVP quarterback, and he definitely had a knack for the game. We dominated the league, winning every game by at least three touchdowns, and I started every game at center. I had no idea that would be the last time I started for the rest of my football career.

I was a tall kid, but I wasn't big. I was never the most talented, but it didn't matter. I absolutely loved the game and was happy to be on the field. Many guys in that league were stronger and tougher than I was, but I didn't mind going against them. Unlike some of my teammates, I wasn't afraid of the physical contact or getting hit.

I also enjoyed the mental aspect of the game. I liked digging in and learning the playbook. I often asked our coach why he called a certain play, so I could learn the strategy behind the game.

In seventh grade, like in youth league, I played offensive line. At that age, it's usually where coaches put guys who can't run, throw, or catch. It definitely wasn't a glamorous position, but I liked it, especially when I played center, where I had to organize the rest of the line.

HIGH SCHOOL

Fall of my freshman year of high school, Dad took me to a home game in Athens. We arrived hours before kickoff and visited the practice field, where a few injured players were signing autographs.

I recognized some of the players and went up to talk to them. One of them was Kregg Lumpkin, a highly touted freshman running back who had already made big contributions to the team. Kregg signed a T-shirt for me, asked what position I played, and then worked with me on my catching technique. I was in awe.

Every experience like this solidified my dream. Still, I didn't share it with anyone—not even my dad. He knew I looked up to the players, but I didn't mention how serious I was about wanting to play. It was a seemingly impossible goal. Being so close to these players in person just confirmed that they were near-perfect physical specimens. They were so big, fast, and strong. The goal of playing with them sounded ridiculous even to me, so I kept it to myself.

In ninth grade, I played on my high school's freshman team. In tenth grade, I moved up to varsity. At my small private school, everyone in tenth through twelfth grade practiced as one team. The guys who didn't play a lot in the varsity games played on JV.

My sophomore year was special. We had a talented senior class led by quarterback Gordon Beckham, who had an arm like a cannon. He later went on to win rookie of the year in Major League Baseball. As of 2018, my sophomore year was the only time Westminster has had a 10-0 football team. We even beat several big schools that were a couple classifications above us.

In high school, I played tight end and linebacker. I was at the bottom of the depth chart, but when we were up by thirty points or more, our coaches emptied the bench and made sure everyone played. Because we were blowing out teams frequently, I played in five games that year. I didn't stay in long, usually half a quarter, but compared to the rest of my football career after seventh grade, that was a good amount of playing time.

My junior year, the team went 4-6, so I didn't have as many opportunities to play, but we did pick up career win number one hundred for our head coach, Gerry Romberg. We also got a new linebacker coach that season, and Kevin Horne became one of my mentors from that point forward. A great player in his own right, Coach Horne was a walk-on member of the University of Tennessee's 1998 national championship team. Coach had our team's respect because he had played at a high level and enjoyed a lot of success. He was also one of the younger coaches, so he could relate to us, and we really looked up to him.

Coach Horne taught me how to tackle properly and how

to embrace contact. I still wasn't very good at tackling, but I really liked the hard-hitting drills, even against guys who were much bigger than I was. I learned that if you shy away from the hits or go in at the wrong angle, you can end up with your head ringing. He also taught me to go hard every time because that's what the other guy is doing.

The coaches did a great job of making everyone on the team feel included, even those of us on the lower end of the depth chart. Everyone did the same drills during practice, whether they were first string or fourth string. At practice, they frequently rotated players, so even fourth-string players had to be ready in case their name was called. And if it was, they had to know where to line up and what to do.

My senior year, we lost the first three games. For the fourth game, the coaches named me captain. I got to walk to midfield and represent my team for the coin toss. We won that game and finished the season on a 5–2 run, bringing our season record to 5–5.

In the final game of my senior season, we built a big lead early in the game. We had the ball at the one-yard line late in the fourth quarter when Coach Gibbons, our offensive coordinator, pulled me aside and said, "Hey, I want you to score this touchdown."

I couldn't believe my ears. I had zero tackles on defense and zero catches on offense over the course of the entire season, but the coach wanted to give me a chance to make a big play to end my high school career.

Coach told me the play and said, "The quarterback isn't looking at any of the other receivers. We're throwing it to you. Do you remember your route?"

"Yes," I replied, trying to play it cool while I was jumping up and down on the inside.

I ran onto the field and joined my teammates in the huddle. Then I lined up at tight end. I kept thinking, *I'd better not drop this!*

When the ball was hiked, I ran three steps and turned. I was wide open, and the throw was accurate. Without having time to think, I held up my hands and caught it. Touchdown! I tossed the ball to the ref and high-fived my teammates, who had run into the end zone to congratulate me. Then I noticed the yellow flag lying on the ground and heard the referee announce a holding penalty against the offense. My one and only score in my entire football career was taken away, just like that.

The ref moved the ball back ten yards to the eleven-yard line. We ran the same play, but the defense had already seen it, so they had me well covered. The quarterback threw it out front, so I could catch it away from the defenders. I dove for the ball, but it was just too far away. Minutes later the clock ran out, ending the season as well as my high school football career.

LOOKING TO COLLEGE

While football didn't come naturally to me, wrestling did. When I was in middle school, I practiced with the high school varsity wrestling team and even beat some of the starters. In high school, I started varsity and qualified for the state wrestling tournament all four years. My junior year, I placed sixth at the state level, and I also made the all-state team.

Wrestling meet during my senior year at Westminster, spring 2007. This photo shows how I was built before I started trying to bulk up for football in college.

Although I was good at wrestling, I didn't love it the way I loved football. I had to ask myself if I would rather wrestle in college, because I was good at it, or play football, because I loved it and was dying to play. Even though playing football at the college level was a much harder goal, I decided to take the more difficult path. That choice made the difference in this story and in the rest of my life.

When it was time to apply to college, I was dead set on attending Georgia. It was actually the only school I applied to, because I couldn't imagine going anywhere else. At one point during my senior year, my academic advisor asked, "Are you sure you don't want to apply anywhere else?"

"No. That's the school I'm going to, so that's the only place I need to apply to."

It would have been easy to stop pursuing football after high school, but my goal hadn't changed. I just had to figure out how to make it happen.

YOUR TURN

The first step in pursuing any goal is figuring out exactly what the goal is in concrete terms. What do you really want to accomplish? You shouldn't have to search too hard. Think of something truly important to you, something you already base your life around, something you look forward to doing, something that's ingrained in you. What comes to mind? Is there a goal you've always dreamed of achieving? Something that has always been in the back of your mind or that you might even be embarrassed to say aloud? It's okay if your goal scares you a little—it should scare you if you are aiming high enough. That's the "impossible" starting place.

CHAPTER 2

THE JOURNEY BEGINS

The only place success comes before work is in the dictionary.

—VINCE LOMBARDI

After being accepted into the University of Georgia in December of my senior year, I turned my attention to the bigger goal: playing football. *How does someone try out for a college football team?* I wondered. *Do I just show up at a coach's office? Is there even such a thing as college football tryouts? How in the world am I going to make this happen?* I didn't know where to start. I tried doing a Google search, but there was no information online—probably intentionally, because coaches don't want random people showing up at practice.

Plus, I was nervous. I imagined one of the first things coaches would ask for is film from my high school days. I had no film. There was no highlight tape. I made one tackle my sophomore year, and even then I was one of three guys tackling the same player. That was it. If the Georgia coaches needed a reference, I could get one; my high school coaches were really nice. But they would also be honest and say I'd never started a game in high school. If I couldn't move forward without a highlight tape, my dream would be shot down immediately.

The summer before my freshman year, I attended a fraternity rush event and ran into a guy who was the kicker for a team I played against in high school. Trent told me he was trying out for the Georgia football team and gave me the name of the coach he had talked to: Coach Tereshinski, the same coach I had met when I was ten years old and attended that Georgia football event with my dad.

Trent was going to a tryout specifically for specialists— punters, kickers, and long snappers—which didn't help me, because I wasn't a specialist. But at least I had some information now: I had the name of the coach in charge of the walk-on program. I didn't tell Trent I was planning to try out. I decided I would just walk into Coach Tereshinski's office right before the specialist tryout and ask when they were having tryouts for other positions.

I was so nervous about talking to Coach T. What if the tryout was already full? I knew colleges recruited a lot of players, more than the number of scholarships available, but I wasn't sure how many places that left on the team for someone like me who wanted to try out.

What if the secretary wouldn't let me into Coach T's office? Or what if he took one look at me and asked me to leave? I weighed 145 pounds. At that weight, trying out for anything other than kicker or punter, let alone linebacker, was dangerous.

The specialist tryout was the day before my first class. I woke up super excited, thinking about how it would feel to tell my parents, sisters, and friends I was trying out—assuming I got the chance to do so.

On the way to Coach T's office, I rehearsed what I would say, trying to avoid going into too much detail about my high school days. I asked the secretary what floor his office was on and then headed for the elevator, hoping Coach T was there and had a couple of minutes to talk.

I walked toward an open elevator, and just as the doors started to close, a hand reached out to hold them open. As I walked in, I saw Coach T standing inside. I immediately recognized him, looking almost exactly the same as when I'd met him eight years earlier. He looked at me for a second, saw that I was in gym clothes, and asked, "Are you the guy I spoke with about the walk-on tryout?"

I nodded, not believing my luck and not wanting to give myself away.

"Come on downstairs. The meeting is about to start."

And just like that, I was in, being walked down to the tryout meeting by Coach T himself. He didn't ask me what position I was trying out for, what my name was, what school I played for, nothing. I just went with it and acted like I was supposed to be there.

We got off the elevator on the first floor of the Butts-Mehre football building. Several guys were standing outside the team meeting room, most of whom were about twice my size.

Coach T punched a code into a keypad near the door and unlocked the meeting room. I followed the other guys inside and then stopped to look around the room. Gigantic graphics were painted on the walls—pictures of famous players throughout Georgia's history. On one wall hung plaques for every SEC championship Georgia had won, and next to those hung plaques for every SEC East division championship and national title. So much football history was displayed in this room, and I was one small step closer to being part of it.

We sat in the leather chairs facing the front of the room

where a large projection screen hung. After everyone was seated, Coach T addressed the group: "You've all expressed interest in trying out for the team. Today we're going to fill out paperwork and discuss the walk-on process. We're allowed to carry 125 players on the roster, and eighty-five of those are on scholarship. That leaves forty walk-on spots, most of which will be filled by preferred walk-ons—players we've recruited out of high school. If we find someone we really like during this tryout, we'll allow them to become a walk-on if there's still room on the roster.

"First, you'll have to get a physical with a team doctor. Once you're cleared, we'll put you through workouts in the weight room. We'll be evaluating you during workouts, which will go through the end of the semester. At that time, we may decide to officially let you try out next spring, which could put you on the team for next fall."

I let that sink in. Basically, Coach T was saying that those of us in the room were competing for a few spots on the team. Actually, at this point, we were competing for an invitation to try out, before the actual tryout.

Coach concluded by saying the roster was full for the current season, but if any spots opened up, some of us might even have the opportunity to join the team within a couple of weeks. That got me excited.

There were about twelve guys in this meeting—a handful of specialists and others who played offense or defense. It was a surprisingly small group, and everyone but me had apparently talked with the coach beforehand. It clearly wasn't a group of random students. I couldn't believe I was sitting here. What were the odds of walking into the building at the exact moment the meeting was about to start? Of being allowed inside when I hadn't spoken to anyone prior to today? I shook my head and smiled.

The paperwork asked for basic information about ourselves, including what position we were trying out for. I thought I would try out for linebacker because that's what I played in youth league, middle school, and high school—I had experience as a linebacker, even if it was as a backup. As I looked around the room, however, I realized I had a lot of work to do. These guys looked like elite athletes, and they were hoping to try out for the team just like I was. I needed to gain a lot of weight, get a ton stronger, and become much faster—in a hurry.

I talked to some of the other walk-ons after the meeting. All of them were high school starters, and some had earned all-state honors. Some had turned down scholarships to Division II schools to be a walk-on at a Division I school like Georgia.

If I had walked into the building just a couple of minutes

later, I would have missed the meeting. I would not have received the information I needed and would not have been included in those workouts. It seemed so surreal. I thought one of the hardest parts would be finding out how to try out and convincing the coaches to give me an opportunity given my size and lack of experience, but here I was with my foot in the door, being handed the information.

Now for the hard part: proving I was worthy of trying out.

REALITY CHECK

During my senior year of high school, our football team had a testing day in the weight room and on the track. The result? I was the weakest player on the team and one of the three slowest. I could bench-press 165 pounds and squat 190. Most guys on my high school team could bench around 300 and squat 350 to 400. There were a significant number of girls on the volleyball and basketball teams who could bench and squat more than I could. I ran the forty-yard dash in 5.6 seconds. That's incredibly slow—about a full second slower than most guys my size. There are 350-pound NFL players who could smoke that number. This was the physical mountain I had to climb to become a Georgia Bulldog.

Given this starting point, I knew I needed to make radical

changes quickly. Immediately after the tryout meeting, I started studying how to put on muscle mass, increase speed, and improve my technique as a linebacker.

The first thing I learned is that I needed to eat more. It's a simple fact that if you eat more calories than your body burns off, you will gain weight. The coaches didn't tell me to bring my weight up; I just knew I was incredibly undersized. I searched the internet for what NFL players and bodybuilders ate if they were trying to gain weight—quality lean muscle mass—and then I put together my own plan. One renowned bodybuilder said he ate six meals a day when he was trying to pack on weight, so I figured that was a good place to start.

Thankfully, Georgia has a great meal plan: four dining halls, including one open 24/7, with no limits on daily visits or the amount of food you can eat. I stayed away from desserts and excessively fatty foods and focused on protein and good carbohydrates: turkey, ground beef, fish, peanut butter and jelly sandwiches, chicken, potatoes, rice, eggs, oatmeal, and more. This meal plan was the exact opposite of what I was used to. I had always eaten three times a day, and during wrestling season, I ate small meals to keep my weight down. Now I was trying to eat as much as possible to bring my weight up.

Eating six times a day requires more planning than the

usual three. My classes started at eight each morning, so I got up in time to be at the dining hall right at seven. My last class ended around eleven each day, and after that I went straight to the dining hall for lunch. I ate again around one or two in the afternoon, and workouts started at three. I ate immediately after my workout and then went back to the dining hall around seven or eight for a regular dinner. About a half hour before bed, I ate one last big meal. After the first few days of my new plan, I constantly felt full. Forcing down that many meals a day wasn't easy, but I knew I had to if I wanted to reach the size needed to play college football.

I also realized I needed to completely rewire the way I approached workouts. In high school, using the weight room was a chore. I didn't enjoy working out, and I was usually sore afterward. However, if I wanted a chance of even trying out for, let alone *making*, the team, I had to make myself love working out as much as I loved practicing. I dedicated myself to researching and learning the most effective exercises and workout structures.

The weight gain happened right away. When I started college in mid-August, I weighed 145. By the end of September, I weighed 160, and by Halloween I was up to 170. I had never tried to gain weight before. At six foot three, I had room to fill out my frame. Any workout I tried and any increase in calories would have probably had the same result at that point. When you're first starting, making that initial progress is easy.

The group of twelve potential walk-ons in the meeting that first day dwindled to six; some guys quit, and a few others were specialists who had already made the team or been cut. The six of us met every Monday, Wednesday, and Friday to train in the football weight room. A graduate assistant named Tyler created the group's workout plan. Each day, we started with heavy compound lifts—squats, front squats, power cleans, or bench press. Then we focused on specific muscle groups: for example, legs one day and chest, shoulders, and triceps the next. Free-weight exercises included shoulder presses, triceps extensions, and bicep curls, as well as pull-ups and push-ups. During this section of the workout, we also incorporated football-centric movements. We used one machine called the jammer, where you crouch in a football stance and then explode upward, pushing your hands away from you. Machines like the jammer don't focus on building muscle mass as much as improving quickness and explosiveness.

We finished our weight-room routine with a couple of machines—on legs day, for example, we might do leg curls to work the hamstrings. After weights, we always ran 40- or 110-yard sprints on the practice field. I was by far the weakest in our group and one of the slowest, but I improved a little each week.

During our workouts, the rest of the team was in the weight room as well. I was awestruck at the weight these players used. I had never seen someone rep out 225 pounds on bench press as if they were holding pipe cleaners in each hand. When they did power cleans, the ground shook after they dropped the bar to the ground. I watched smaller guys squat more than 400 pounds for several reps. I couldn't believe how big and strong everyone was.

In addition to working out three days a week with the group hoping to try out, I worked out two days on my own. The other guys were so far ahead of me that if I only improved at the same rate as everyone else, I would still be behind. I needed to do more.

During my personal Tuesday and Thursday workouts, I focused on a different muscle group than we had worked the day before. If we did squats on Monday, I would work arms on Tuesday. In my personal workouts, I focused solely on true weight lifting to build muscle mass. I was getting the explosiveness training on the other days; plus, I didn't have access to football machines like the jammer. Whatever muscle group I was working, I hammered it so that I was sore at the end.

A couple of weeks into fall workouts, Coach T told three of the guys in our group that he was impressed with their performance and the team had room for them to start practicing immediately. They joined the team as walk-ons, and our group was reduced to three: Tyler Williamson, Brian Pelon, and me. Tyler was a preferred walk-on with a guaranteed spot, but he'd suffered an injury his senior year of high school and wasn't cleared to practice yet. Brian had played at a small private high school and dreamed of playing for Georgia like I did. We ended up becoming roommates my sophomore year and, to this day, Brian is one of my closest friends.

Like me, Brian and Tyler were intent on improving, so we developed a friendly competition. Each week, we tried to break our personal best in weight or reps, becoming a little stronger than we were the week before.

During one workout, there weren't enough bench-press stations to go around, so we needed to work in with other groups—guys who were actually on the team.

I saw a group of three at a bench press, so I walked over.

"Can I work in?" I asked the guy closest to me.

"Sure," he said. When he looked up, I almost gasped. It was Kregg Lumpkin, now a fifth-year senior. The same guy who had thrown the ball around with me when Dad and I visited the practice field. I still had the T-shirt he signed for me four years earlier.

"Thanks," I replied.

I stood to the side and watched Kregg take his turn. I looked at the number of plates, did a quick calculation, and realized he was repping out 285. *Oh my gosh. I am so much weaker than these guys!*

When it was my turn, I walked up to the bar. Kregg knew I wasn't going to be able to lift what he had and started taking off plates. He was cool about it; he could probably tell I was embarrassed. He stopped when we took the weight down to 185. I quickly did my reps, put the plates back on the bar for the next person, and waited for my next set.

That day was a huge reality check. I had gotten this far, but man, I had a long way to go.

THE 2007 SEASON

While I was preparing to try out that fall, the Bulldogs were having a great season. After beating Oklahoma State, they lost a couple of games and came into the matchup against Florida with a 5-2 record. Florida is Georgia's biggest rival, and bragging rights are always at stake. That year was no different, especially because Florida was the reigning national champ, ranked in the top ten, and had Tim Tebow at quarterback.

In his team speech before the game, head coach Mark Richt told the players, "When we get our first score, I want the whole team to celebrate." He meant that he wanted everyone *on the sidelines* jumping up and down. What happened was that the entire team—all sixty-five guys— ran into the *end zone* and started jumping up and down. The team went crazy. They received multiple penalties, but it was worth it. They went on to win the game 42–30, out-dueling Tebow, who won the Heisman later that year.

Two weeks later, the team faced Auburn, another big rival. Coach Richt told the fans to wear black, prompting people to wonder if the team would wear black jerseys, something they hadn't done in decades.

The team wore red jerseys during pregame warm-ups and then went back into the locker room for one last pep talk. Then, with AC/DC's "Back in Black" blasting through the loudspeakers, the team burst through the banner wearing black jerseys instead of red, and the crowd went nuts. The momentum from that opening, as well as a fast start on the field, carried the team through the game, and they ended up scoring twenty-eight unanswered points to win 45–20.

Georgia finished the year with a Sugar Bowl win and a number-two ranking. It was the eleventh straight year Georgia finished in the top twenty-five, the longest active streak of any team in the country at the time. This was the team I was working out with in the weight room. This was the team I was hoping to try out for.

DECISION TIME

After one workout at the end of the semester, Coach T asked Brian and me to come up to his office. I knew this was it—the moment of truth. I was nervous and wondered if I had done enough to earn a tryout. Was this the end of the line or my golden opportunity?

Coach T sat behind his desk while Brian and I stood, waiting to hear his decision.

"I've seen you guys work out this fall," he said. "I'll be honest. At the beginning I doubted you would make it through those workouts, but you both worked hard and showed improvement. I've decided to let you both try out for the team this spring. We'll have a meeting in January right after class starts—Brian, is everything all right?"

Next to me, Brian had turned a little pale. I felt like I looked the same way, but Coach didn't seem to notice.

"I'm all right; we just worked out hard," Brian replied. I could tell he was as excited as I was that we were getting to try out.

"Well, you can lie down and put your feet up if you need to," Coach said.

And that's exactly what Brian did. He lay down on the carpet and put his feet up on a chair.

Coach continued, "Okay, you guys need to stay in shape over winter break. In January, you'll have more of the same workouts and conditioning with the team. In February, we have mat drills. Those are going to test you harder than anything you've ever done. In March, the team will start practicing, and in April, you'll have the spring game. After that, we'll make decisions about who to keep and who to cut. But just know coaches can cut people at any point in the spring." He may have said more, but I was too excited to listen.

After Coach finished, we both thanked him and calmly left his office. Once we were outside the building, we high-fived, so excited we could barely contain it. I knew only Brian could appreciate how I felt, having gone through those workouts together for the last few months.

As excited as I was, I knew that we were in store for a

much greater challenge in the spring. It's one thing to lift weights next to the scholarship players. It's something entirely different to put on pads and hit them in a drill.

YOUR TURN

After you identify what you want to achieve, you have to figure out how to get there. A seemingly impossible goal can appear overwhelming if you only look at the big picture. It helps to break the overall goal into more manageable steps, creating a roadmap for yourself.

For me, making the football team was too broad and general. That was the end result I wanted, but I needed to identify specific actions to get there. These fell into three main areas: eating, working out/running, and position-specific training. After identifying these areas, I broke them down even further: What do I need to eat and how often? What kind of exercises develop speed? What techniques do successful linebackers use? I knew if I just woke up each day and focused on those three areas, I would continue to improve and push forward toward the bigger goal of making the team.

The way you attack your goal doesn't have to be glamorous or flashy. It doesn't have to be complicated. It just has to be consistent and focused on the right things that will deliver results. Eating right, exercising, doing football drills—these aren't rocket science. They're just the basics I needed to execute consistently if I wanted to improve and become a Bulldog.

Revisit the goal you set at the end of chapter 1. What specific, practical steps do you need to accomplish each day to get there?

--- **CHAPTER 3** ---

THE TRYOUT

Success is not owned. It is leased and rent is due every day.

—J. J. WATT

Beep. Beep. Beep. I hit the alarm and looked at the clock: 3:45 a.m. I jumped out of bed, simultaneously excited and anxious. I got dressed and walked over to the student gym.

I didn't really know what to expect from mat drills; we were purposely not given many details. I knew they were at 4:30 a.m., three days a week, for the month of February. I knew that I would be doing a lot of running, and I'd heard rumors that they were a nightmare. Several veteran players told me mat drills were the toughest thing they had ever done.

I arrived fifteen minutes early; I definitely didn't want

to start off by being late. By 4:30, the whole team was there—scholarship players, walk-ons, and guys like me who were trying out. The strength coach gathered us all together for a quick talk.

"Good morning, everyone. Mat drills are meant to evaluate your mental toughness. We want a fast and physical team, so you need to be fast and physical during mat drills. You will be graded on every single drill. If you get a thumbs-up, you will wait for the next rep to begin. If you get a thumbs-down, you'll run back to the start and immediately go again. Let's warm up."

After twenty minutes of stretching, push-ups, and jogging, the strength coach dismissed us to our first station. My group of forty-some guys went to the running station, which turned out to be the easiest of the three. At the end of twenty minutes, the coach blew his whistle and the whole team rotated; my group went to the mat next. The dreaded mat.

We lined up in groups of five on a wrestling mat. The starters went first, and I watched intently so I would know what was coming. Finally, it was my group's turn. The five of us got into a football stance facing the coaches. When the group ahead of us cleared out of the way, we started chopping our feet. After the coach blew his whistle, we all dove onto the mat and immediately pushed ourselves up and back into a football stance. We started chopping our feet, and when the coach pointed left, we all shuffled left. He pointed right, and we shuffled right. Then left. Right. Left. He pointed down and we hit the mat, quickly got up, and sprinted to the next coach, who had us chop our feet while he walked back and forth in front of us. Finally, he blew his whistle, and we sprinted through the finish line. At the end, we looked to the coach for the sign. It was thumbs-down, so the five of us sprinted back to the start line and waited our turn to repeat the drill: football stance, on the mat, on our feet, quick steps. This time instead of shuffling right and left, the coach had us barrel-roll to the right, get on our feet in a football stance, and barrel-roll to the left before chopping our feet and sprinting to the end. After we finished the rep, we looked to the coach: thumbs-down. Back to the starting line.

My group wasn't the only one getting a thumbs-down. Everyone did the first two times around. The coaches wanted to send a clear message: none of you are perfect and you all need to work harder. It quickly became apparent that the mat station was really about testing how far everyone was willing to push to make themselves and the team better.

Just before my group stepped up to the line for the third time, there was a holdup. One of the groups ahead of us had received their third thumbs-down. On the way back to the starting point, one of the scholarship guys veered left, ran over to the trash can, and vomited. Players and coaches started yelling at him.

"Hurry up!"

"Come on. Get back in line!"

Then the trainer stepped in and said, "No, he's done." After the player had gathered himself, he walked with the trainer to a side area, where he was evaluated and given some water.

A few reps later, a handful of exhausted players took themselves out of the drill and joined the first guy off to the side. At our next water break, I glanced at those who were out for the day. Some were walk-ons who were already on the team. Some were five-star recruits who almost every school in the country had fought over. Some were on the all-conference team. It was the first time I truly saw these guys as equals. They were all flesh and blood, just like me.

This realization gave me a glimmer of hope: despite the seeming impossibility of the goal and my obvious short-comings in speed and strength, achieving it might really be possible. Now I just had to get through the rest of mat drills and spring practice.

JANUARY

After my meeting with Coach T in December, the semester ended and everyone took exams. The football team started preparing for the bowl game, but since Brian and I weren't part of that, we headed home for a few weeks.

When we came back to Athens, Coach T held a meeting with everyone who would be trying out that spring. More than forty people showed up this time—a lot more than the previous fall—including several midyear transfers.

"All right, I know y'all are wondering about the tryout process," Coach T said. "It has several steps that I will walk you through now. You need to understand that anytime during this process, you can be cut. Even preferred walk-ons we recruited can be cut after their first season. Everything depends on how much room we have at each position. We will have team workouts and conditioning all month; the workout groups are split up into skill players, big skill, and linemen. If we think you have what it takes, we will let you continue into mat drills in February. They will start at 4:30 in the morning and are on Wednesday, Friday, and Saturday. If you show up even a minute late, you will be cut. If you can't complete a drill or have to stop to get sick, you will be cut.

"If you complete mat drills, you will stop by the equipment room so they can fit you for pads and set you up with a locker. Spring practice runs for four weeks and ends with the G-Day game in early April. You will be thrown into your position group and expected to compete and learn the playbook. After the spring game, we will make cuts to trim the roster so we won't have more than 125 guys total on the team.

"Gentlemen, it takes a special kind of man to be a walk-on. You have to be willing to fight every day to keep your spot on this team. It is thankless work; you won't be the ones starting for us on Saturdays, but we still need you to give your best in practice. I have seen years where ten guys from this tryout group make the team and years where nobody makes it. Very few guys who make the team will ever get to play in a game. If you don't think this is for you, just let me know and I won't hold it against you."

After Coach finished outlining the process, he went over the GPA requirements for those trying out. Several guys didn't meet them and had to leave the room immediately.

I knew the tryout process was going to be tough, but Coach T's words magnified how many hurdles I had to cross to successfully make the team. At any point on any day in any workout or practice, I could be cut and my dream would come to an end.

The day after classes resumed, we started team workouts.

These were basically the same as the fall workouts I had been doing with Brian and Tyler, but now the whole team was involved. During the season, players focus more on injury prevention and flexibility. In January, however, the whole team shifts gears to focus on strength training in preparation for next year.

Although my lifting routine followed basically the same structure as it had in the fall, being in the weight room felt different in January. Instead of a grad student leading workouts, the head strength coach, Dave Van Halanger, oversaw the program. Instead of training with a group of three, I trained with the whole team, and we were all focused on the same goal: getting bigger, faster, and stronger.

The three groups for workouts were skill, big skill, and linemen. The skill group included the smallest, fastest guys: running backs, safeties, cornerbacks, and wide receivers. The big skill group, which I was in, included tight ends, fullbacks, quarterbacks, and linebackers. The linemen group included the offensive and defensive linemen—the biggest guys on the team.

After we split up, Keith Gray, who was in charge of workouts for the big skill group, went over the structure of workouts and the conditioning schedule. We would work out Monday through Thursday from three to five.

Everyone scheduled morning classes so we were finished around noon. By two o'clock, we were heading to the football facility to get ready for meetings.

FEBRUARY

After a month of strength-building workouts, our schedule changed. For the month of February, we had mat drills three days a week and strength training two other days.

Everyone was required to wear the same thing to mat drills: gray Georgia football shorts and a black T-shirt with the team goals written in the shape of a pyramid: win our division, win our conference, and win the national championship. There was one difference for those of us trying out: since no one knew who we were, we all had to write our name on a piece of painter's tape and stick it to the front of our shirt.

Mat drills involved six exercises spread out over three stations—running, agility, and the mat. Each station lasted twenty minutes. When time expired, the coach blew his whistle, and everyone sprinted from one station to the next. There was no rest between stations. As soon as everyone arrived, the next drill began.

Starting the first day, I wanted to give maximum effort on every rep. I didn't want to give the coaches a reason to cut me on the spot, which later happened to several people. If a scholarship player or walk-on who was already on the team fell out of the drill, they were finished for the day. If someone trying out did so, they were finished, period. There were already more guys out there than the team had room for. Coaches understood that you may not be as athletic or strong as the scholarship guys, but there was no excuse to be out of shape, and they didn't have time to coach up fitness.

We proceeded through each station in the same groups we had for workouts—skill, big skill, and linemen. The running station involved two drills: the rope drill and the ladder. At the rope drill, five players lined up together and ran in place for about ten seconds, bringing their knees up to waist height on each step—high enough to reach the rope the coaches were holding. At the end of ten seconds, they sprinted about ten yards to the finish line. Then the next group did the same thing. If our entire group of five didn't complete the drill satisfactorily, we finished the sprint and got back in line to repeat the drill while everyone else waited for the next round. We did about twelve rounds in ten minutes, but if your group got sent back a couple of times, you could end up doing more. I figured as long as I was pushing hard each time, sprinting through the finish line, and not standing out in a bad way effort-wise, I would be fine.

The other running drill was the ladder, which focused on

quick footwork—moving forward, backward, and side to side through a ladder laid out on the ground by planting each foot between the "rungs." It was almost like a sewing machine: your feet moved through the ladder in a quick and repetitive up-and-down pattern. In this drill, all eyes were on each person individually because we ran through the ladder one at a time. If you touched any part of the ladder, you had to finish that rep and then immediately repeat the drill. If you went too slowly and the guy behind you caught up, you would be sent back.

I felt a lot of pressure in this drill; I had to be fast and there was no room for error. I kept my eyes on my feet, making sure my body stayed in rhythm—smooth, evenly paced, and quick. I knew if I made one misstep, everyone would see and I would be sent back. I blocked out everything going on around me and focused. Right foot in, left foot in. Right foot out, left foot out. Repeat on the next rung. Quick, precise. No lazy steps that snag the ladder. After each successful trip through the ladder, we got back in line and waited to do it again. We kept going until the ten minutes expired.

The agility station was broken up into three exercises, so we spent about seven minutes at each one. First was the high rope ladder. This ladder wasn't as long as the one at the running station, but it was about a foot above the ground, which meant we had to step high and be really precise. After going through the last rung, we sprinted to the end line. If we touched any part of the ladder, we finished the sprint and got back in line to repeat the drill. If we made it through successfully, we waited to the side until everyone got a thumbs-up.

The second agility exercise was the chute, a four-foot-high red metal frame with a breathable black tarp stretched across the top. One by one, we ran into the chute and chopped our feet, crouching low so we didn't hit our heads. Coaches gave directions on whether we moved forward, backward, or sideways while squatting in the chute. The chute drill was a test of focus during agony: chopping my feet and moving laterally while staying that low required ignoring the shooting pain in my tired legs.

The third agility drill was the pro shuttle. We were put into groups of three and stood one in front of the other, facing the coach. If he pointed right, we all shuffled to the right cone and touched it. If he pointed left, we shuffled to the left cone. We had to watch him the whole time and respond to his nonverbal commands. When the coach pointed behind himself, we sprinted ten yards through the end line. If anyone went the wrong way, moved too slowly, or did anything else the coach found unsatisfactory, he sent the whole group back to the starting point to repeat the drill.

The final station was the mat, from which this whole February training period gets its name. The drill had a lot of moving parts and coordinated movements. I didn't see one group go through the entire drill without being sent back at least once. People were doing well if they only got sent back twice during the twenty minutes at the station. Sometimes the coaches sent groups back three or four times in a row, just to make a point or to see how mentally tough the guys were. If a group was sent back three times in a row, they might be the only group still going, in which case they would have to run back and start again immediately.

The mat is truly a revealing experience. When people are pushed to the brink, you get to see who they really are. You see which guys will fight when it gets tough and which guys will give up.

I didn't work out on my own in February, since team workouts and mat drills now covered five days a week. When I wasn't in class or with the team, I made sure to rest, hydrate, and eat healthy.

By the end of mat drills, the original group of more than forty guys trying out had dwindled to thirty-four. After factoring in the new class of preferred walk-ons who would arrive in June, that meant thirty-four guys were trying out for roughly six spots. I made it through mat drills, but now I needed to prove myself on the field.

MARCH

On the last day of mat drills, everyone was measured for shoulder pads and helmets in preparation for the upcoming spring practice. When I walked into the equipment room for the first time, I was blown away. It looked like a massive Nike outlet stocked with University of Georgia gear. One aisle had tables filled with hundreds of pairs of brand-new cleats. Another aisle had just gloves, and another had stacks of black-and-white Nike Dri-FIT shirts. In one corner stood a rack of game jerseys. Any kind of football-related clothing and equipment you could think of—they had it.

We were assigned lockers on the first day of spring practice. There were so many people trying out that we had to double up. Sharing a locker was a constant reminder of the position I was in: there wasn't enough room for all of us, and by the end of April, many of us would be cut.

Before each practice, we held position-group meetings where each coach would review film from previous practices. Then we headed out to the practice field.

I was excited and nervous about being on the field with these guys. Was I physical enough to be out there? The practice field is where the team prepares for games, sorts out the depth chart, and determines who's going to make the team. Although the January workouts and

February mat drills were important, the field was where I was really going to sink or swim. At the end of the day, we were football players, not professional weight lifters, so on-the-field, game-situation practice was the most important part.

We practiced three to four days a week during the month of March. We arrived around 2:30 to put on pads. From 3:00 to 4:30 we had position meetings to watch film and then went out to practice, which consisted of a twenty-minute warm-up followed by special teams and position work. Practice itself lasted about two and a half hours, so it was usually around five hours from the time we arrived until the time we left each day.

Spring practice involved many drills I'd done in high school, but they were executed at a higher level because the players were so much bigger, faster, and stronger. Some players were among the top-ten recruits at their position in the whole country. One of them was Rennie Curran, a linebacker who helped me learn some of the plays.

We did a lot of bag drills, block-shedding drills, and tackling drills. Bag drills were similar to the ladder in mat drills: we shuffled sideways, forward, and backward between bags. The goal was to work on quick footwork while keeping our eyes on the field and a ready stance. In block-shedding drills, one player was on offense; the other player was a linebacker trying to get separation and maintain the gap he was responsible for. In another drill, one guy acted as a running back and the other was a linebacker practicing form tackling. To avoid injury, during most spring practices we stopped short of tackling to the ground; we just wrapped up the ballcarrier or tagged off with two hands.

Going one-on-one in a drill against Rennie Curran during my first tryout, March 2008. Linebacker coach John Jancek is standing behind us.

We had an acclimation period for the first few days of spring practice, during which we wore our jersey, shorts, and helmet without pads. Then we added shoulder pads for a few days, and finally full pads. Even then, we only tackled to the ground for about twenty minutes of each practice. During the regular season, the full-tackle window is even smaller.

During spring practice, I kept up with my six-meals-a-day plan. Brian often joined me in the dining hall, as did Craig Sager Jr., son of the legendary NBA sideline reporter, who was also trying out that spring. Every day after practice, we chowed down, trying to replenish the calories we had just burned. Steak or shrimp stir-fry with rice, baked chicken, mashed potatoes—whatever we could eat that was high in protein and complex carbs. All three of us were trying to put on weight, so we ate a lot.

The week before the spring game, we practiced inside Sanford Stadium. That was my first time entering the stadium as a player. As I walked onto the field, I looked up in awe. The place was massive. The stands were empty and we were just scrimmaging against ourselves, but it was still exciting. Here I was, scrimmaging on the field, trying out to be a Georgia football player. I was one step closer. The coaches rotated everyone into the scrimmage, giving all of us—including the guys trying out—a chance to play.

On my second play, the defensive lineman in front of me was pushed to the side by two offensive linemen, creating a gap. The running back got the handoff and ran through the hole, straight for me. I ran forward, hit his legs, and brought him to the ground. It felt like it was happening in slow motion. It was my first tackle since my sophomore year of high school, and it was in Sanford Stadium.

APRIL

By the end of March, I was more comfortable with the drills and I had grown stronger, but I was still slower than the other guys and nowhere near as big. I had finally bench-pressed 225 pounds for the first time, but most of the other linebackers could bench 225 fifteen times. They were maxing out at well over 300.

Soon enough, it was time for the spring game—the culmination of our tryout. After this game, I would know if I had made the team.

For G-Day, the whole team, including coaches, was divided into two teams: the red and black. The goal was to make it feel as much like a real game as possible.

With Brian Pelon before the spring game during our freshman year, April 2008.

A few hours before kickoff, we had a pregame meal with family and friends in the basketball coliseum. My parents and sisters came into town for G-Day, and I was sitting with them chatting when I felt a tug on my jersey. I turned around and saw a boy in a Bulldogs T-shirt holding out a Georgia jersey and pen. He could have been me ten years earlier.

"Hey, will you sign this?" he asked.

"Sure," I said as I took the pen and signed his jersey.

"Thank you," he said, and then moved on to the next guy. He clearly had no idea who I was or that I was only trying out for the team, but it was a special moment nonetheless. No one had ever asked me for an autograph. Just a few years earlier, I was the one asking Georgia football players for autographs.

After lunch I said good-bye to my family. They went to find their seats, and I went to get ready. Hanging in my shared locker was a game jersey. It didn't have my name on it, but it was an actual Bulldogs game jersey, and it was mine. As I put on my pads and uniform, I thought about what a milestone this was. It was the culmination of my four-month tryout. I spent the last few minutes flipping through my playbook and asking Darryl Gamble and Darius Dewberry a few questions, making sure I knew what I was supposed to do in each situation. Even though I didn't get many reps in practice, I was expected to know my assignment for every play. This was my last chance to make a big impression.

Just before game time, we headed into the team locker room inside Sanford Stadium instead of the locker room in the football facility we had been using for the past four months. I had never been in this locker room. Whiteboards hung on the walls, one board for each position group, with semicircles of chairs in front of each board. In the middle of the floor was the Georgia G logo. I walked to my position group and took a seat. I couldn't believe I was in here.

As you exit the locker room toward the field, there's a sign above the door that says, "Be worthy as you run upon this hallowed sod, for you dare to tread where champions have trod." I thought about the Heisman Trophy winners who had called this field home. I was about to play on the same field. The football fan in me was blown away, but I knew I needed to focus on the task at hand.

I ran onto the field with my teammates. The stadium was only about 40 percent full, but the crowd still cheered loudly as we entered.

The game itself was a defensive affair. At halftime, my

team—the red team—was up 17-3. In the locker room, Coach Jancek, the linebacker coach, reviewed the first half and discussed changes we would make in the second half. He then looked at me and two other walk-on hopefuls and said, "You guys are going in for the first series."

I couldn't believe my ears. I hadn't known whether I'd get to play in this game. I reached down to grab my helmet and looked over at the defensive line, Brian's group. He gave me a thumbs-up, letting me know he was getting in the game. I nodded to tell him I was, too.

Back on the field, I stood near Brian and the other guys who were going in. When it was our turn, we ran onto the field and joined the huddle, waiting to hear the play. I lined up at Will linebacker, who was responsible for the weak side. The three plays called by the offense all went to the strong side or to a receiver I wasn't covering, so I didn't get to make a tackle. The offense punted, and that was the end of my spring game debut. It was a quick series, but a successful one. No one scored in the second half, so the final score remained 17-3.

After the spring game, I felt a tempered optimism about my chances of making the team. I had made it through mat drills, even though some other guys couldn't. I knew I had improved, but I also knew a lot of guys still had me beat in size, strength, and skill, plus the coaches were only

going to take a few people from the tryout group. Would
I be one of them?

YOUR TURN

In the sci-fi movie *Gattaca*, society has accepted genetic modification to give parents the choice between having children by traditional means and using modification to eliminate the odds of genetic disorders. When Vincent is born naturally, he is given a high probability of having several disorders and a life expectancy of only thirty years. Regretting their decision, Vincent's parents decide to use genetic modification for their next son, Anton.

As the movie progresses, the brothers play an ongoing game of chicken where they swim as far as they can into the ocean and the one who turns around first loses. The genetically superior Anton always wins. Then one day, Vincent challenges Anton and pushes himself to keep going, commenting, "Something was very different about that day. Every time Anton tried to pull away, he found me right beside him. Until finally, the impossible happened." Vincent then sees Anton drowning and turns around to save him. Vincent says, "It was the one moment in our lives where my brother was not as strong as he believed, and I was not as weak. It was the moment that made everything else possible." Vincent realizes he has something that could make up for his physical weakness—that his mental toughness could close the gap for what he lacks in strength, speed, and endurance.

Later in the movie, Anton challenges Vincent to another game of chicken. As they're swimming, Anton asks, "How are you doing this, Vincent? How have you done any of this?"

"This is how I did it, Anton: I never saved anything for the swim back," Vincent replies. With that, Anton realizes Vincent will not give up until he wins, and he turns back to the shore in defeat.

In many ways, I felt like Vincent—a normal guy surrounded by genetically superior athletes. They could easily do things I would never be able to do. Like Vincent, however, I knew that it's possible to outwork anyone, no matter how talented they are. That's why I put in extra workouts on my own while the rest of the team was relaxing. That's why I ate so many healthy, structured meals while some of the guys skipped breakfast and had pizza, hot wings, and Coke for lunch and dinner.

My moment was when I saw the elite scholarship player puke into the trash can on the first day of mat drills. All of a sudden, I realized he and the other scholarship guys were human, not invincible, and that no amount of talent could save them from mat drills, where the battle is fought in the mind. That was the day that made everything else possible; I had a glimpse into a way I could make this team even though I was lacking in many areas. With each player who got sick or couldn't finish the drills, I grew stronger, knowing that, even if only in this one small aspect of the tryout, I could do something others could not.

Think about your own goal and what you need to attain it. Do you feel overwhelmed by what you lack in knowledge, skills, or experience? Think of areas where you excel, no matter how seemingly small, and write them down next to your goal. Let those successes keep you motivated when the journey gets tough, and be relentless in your pursuit. It is your responsibility, not anyone else's, to achieve your goal. Find a way to leverage your strengths to get you closer to your dream.

CHAPTER 4

THE REBOUND

It is the act of failing that makes you improve, that makes you want to do better, that makes you want more out of yourself.

—JARET GROSSMAN, "FAILURE BEFORE SUCCESS,"
A YOUTUBE VIDEO BY MUSCLE PRODIGY

A week after the spring game, we were back to workouts and running. I was still riding high from the experience of playing in Sanford Stadium. At the end of the first workout, we went to the practice field and ran 110-yard sprints. Craig and I were torching the other guys in our group. Since we weren't guaranteed a spot, we were probably taking it far more seriously, but still—it felt good to be leading our group, given how slow I had been four months earlier.

On the second day back in the weight room, I started with power cleans. Brian and I warmed up with 155, then moved to 199 and 221. Brian went first at 221 and nailed it. Then I did three reps back-to-back, a new personal best. As I high-fived Brian, assistant strength coach Clay Walker walked by and said, "Cook, I didn't know you could do that much."

"I can now," I said with a grin.

Brian and I gathered our stuff and moved to the bench press. We were putting weight on the bar when Coach T walked into the weight room and called out several names, including mine and Brian's. "Come see me in my office," Coach said.

My stomach clenched. I didn't look at Brian, but I knew he was thinking the same thing I was: *This is it.*

When we got to his office, Coach addressed the ten to twelve walk-ons in front of him. "I appreciate the hard work you guys put in the last few months. You've really transformed your bodies. But there are very few spots open, and we've decided to go with other guys."

With that, our tryout was over and we were dismissed. I felt so disappointed.

As we left the room, Brian and I were silent. We walked back to the locker room to grab our stuff. Finally, I asked, "Do you want to go eat?"

"Yeah, sure."

This is what we did after every workout and practice, so we went to the dining hall to eat and digest the news. We both felt down that we had gotten cut, but we decided to give it another shot. After all, we were freshmen and had a lot of time left to improve.

SUMMER IN ATHENS

Receiving that news in the middle of a workout and minutes after setting a personal best on power clean was rough. It hurt. But I refused to give up. My goal hadn't changed; I just needed to refine my strategy.

After the spring game, there were only a few weeks left in the semester. I spent that time working out in the regular student gym and continuing my eating plan. I also made an honest assessment of where I stood. I pretended I was a coach and asked myself several questions: Am I really an SEC-level football player? No. Am I strong enough? No. Had I done well enough in mat drills? Yes. My answers showed me where I needed to focus: I had the mental toughness, but I just wasn't physically tough enough to make it happen. I needed to get bigger, faster, and stronger. Though I had made it through mat drills, those skills hadn't translated on the field into the quickness and strength I needed to make the team.

Before I got cut, I received a copy of the football summer-workout plan. I decided to follow the team workouts plus some. They were working out four days a week, so I would work out six. I also started eating more. During mat drills and practice, I burned so many calories that I couldn't put on weight, so I was still at 185. I figured if I added a seventh meal over the summer, that would help me bulk up.

Brian and I both stayed at school that summer, which made training more fun and competitive. I took a job as a server and focused on working out, eating, and becoming the best football player *I* could be. I realized if I always compared myself to a starter who could squat 500, I would become discouraged, but if I compared myself to where I had been the week before, I had a realistic number to beat and a sense of accomplishment when I did so. By the end of June, I squatted 315 for the first time ever. Improvements like this strengthened me mentally as well as physically, which was crucial to achieving my goal. In order to succeed, I had to truly *know* that I had improved enough to earn a spot on the team, and with each day it became a little bit easier to believe.

FALL OF SOPHOMORE YEAR

By the time school started in August, I had gained fifteen pounds. I was now up to two hundred, far more than I had ever weighed, but still small for a college linebacker.

Even though I started the school year bigger and stronger than the year before, I still had a lot of work to do. This time around, I knew what waited for me in the spring and what I had to do to be ready. I started by setting a goal for getting bigger: gain two pounds a week over the course of the fall semester. Since semesters are sixteen weeks long, meeting that goal would put me at 232 by December, which is right at what most SEC linebackers weigh. Then I would just have to match their strength and speed.

My friend Craig had officially made the team and even got to dress out for the first game. Georgia debuted at number one in the country to start the 2008 season.

I went to every home game that fall, and they all held new meaning for me. I still got as excited about games as I had when I was a kid, but it was different. I knew those guys; I had trained with them and practiced against them. I understood what went on behind the scenes. It was bittersweet, however, because I was in the stands while they were on the field. I knew I had a lot more to accomplish if I wanted to be out there with the team.

THE STRONGEST DAWG

With Craig going through fall practice, Brian and I added a friend named Winston Leon to our workout group. Winston was going to try out as cornerback the next spring.

Together we created our own training program that involved lifting six days a week and running four days.

We also gave ourselves a short-term goal, something to focus on before spring tryouts. Every year, the University of Georgia has a school powerlifting competition called the Strongest Dawg, and we decided to compete. Just over a year earlier, I would have never signed up for this, but since then I had completely flipped my mindset about lifting and had learned to enjoy the hard work. Plus, I was seeing steady improvement in my strength, which motivated me to keep pushing myself.

The Strongest Dawg fit right in with all the powerlifting and bodybuilding research I'd been doing. Animal Pak's website in particular had helpful articles on what famous bodybuilders and powerlifters had done to put on lean muscle mass. I watched movies like *Pumping Iron*, the Arnold Schwarzenegger documentary, and *Cost of Redemption*, about Ronnie Coleman, who won the Mr. Olympia title eight years in a row.

The Strongest Dawg took place in mid-October. By then I weighed 214, which put me at the low end of the 230 weight class. The competition consisted of three lifts: bench press, squat, and dead lift. Winners were determined by the cumulative weight lifted over the three events.

In bench press, the three of us all posted numbers that were about what we expected. I maxed out at 275, which was a definite improvement; the previous spring, my max was 225. I also squatted a personal best of 375, up eighty pounds from the spring.

For me, the competition came down to the last challenge: the dead lift. I was either going to win my weight class with a new personal best or go home empty-handed. Everyone had three attempts. My first lift was 405 pounds, which I had done before and felt easy. Then I lifted 435 on my second attempt. On my third attempt I lifted 465, far more than I had ever done before. I not only won my weight class, but I ended up having the highest dead lift of the day out of all weight classes.

The Strongest Dawg competition, October 2008. I deadlifted 465, a personal best that helped me win my weight class.

If I hadn't done the Strongest Dawg, I probably wouldn't have progressed as quickly in my size and strength. Having Brian and Winston with me, working on the same lifts and training toward the same goal, really helped. We all remembered what each person lifted, so we were held accountable to put on a little more weight each week. They weren't eating seven meals a day, but I could count on them to be there for three or four of them.

REQUESTING ANOTHER TRYOUT

In order to keep up the pace of gaining two pounds a week, in late fall I had to increase to eight full-sized meals. I was eating roughly every two hours from the time I woke up to the time I went to bed. I would get up at 6:45 a.m. and eat at 7:00. When my first class ended around 9:30, I would eat, and then again around 11:30, 1:30, 4:00, 6:00, 8:00, and 10:00. Weekends were easier because I didn't have to work around classes. I also carried around a gallon jug of water; it sort of became my trademark. Random people would walk by and say, "Hey, it's the guy with the water jug." When you're eating that much food, you need to stay hydrated. I definitely got some weird looks, but it didn't bother me.

After the Strongest Dawg, I kept gaining weight at a rate of two pounds a week. By the last week of the semester, I hit my goal, weighing exactly 232. I had gained thirty-two pounds in less than four months.

I also kept getting stronger: whereas last spring I'd bench-pressed 225 once, I could now rep out multiples. One week it was three times, the next week it was five, and then six. A few weeks later I hit eight.

By the time December rolled around, I felt ready to try out. Whereas the year before I didn't even know where to start, now I knew the steps to take, including the person to talk to. I walked to the football building and found Coach T in the hallway leading up to his office.

"How can I help you?" Coach asked.

"I'd like to try out for the team," I said.

"Yeah, of course. We'll have a meeting in January. I'll see you then." There was no hesitation in his reply.

I don't know if he recognized me. It's possible he didn't, since I looked nothing like the 145-pound guy who had walked into his office the year before.

Just like that, I was granted a second tryout.

YOUR TURN

Your journey toward a goal is bound to have obstacles; it's part of the process. The key is how you handle those setbacks. When I was told there wasn't room for me on the team, I could have easily stopped pursuing my goal. I saw how big those guys were, how much faster they could run, and how much weight they could lift. I knew my goal sounded crazy. Instead, I got back up and kept moving forward because my objective hadn't changed. If you really want that goal, you have to keep pushing through the inevitable bumps in the road.

How do you respond to obstacles and setbacks? Do you give up or try again? Do you make excuses for why it won't work, or do you look for ways to get around the roadblock? Don't get angry for the sake of getting angry; instead, channel your frustration into something constructive that moves you toward your goal. In addition, don't be afraid to reach out to others when you hit an obstacle. Learn from people who are more experienced or have faced the same challenge themselves.

CHAPTER 5

ANOTHER CHANCE

It ain't about how hard you hit. It's about how hard you can get hit and keep moving forward; how much you can take and keep moving forward. That's how winning is done.

—ROCKY BALBOA

In January 2009, I walked into the football weight room for the first time since I had been cut. I felt excited for another opportunity, nervous because I knew the level of competition I was up against, and ready to be training with the team again.

I spotted Clay Walker, an assistant strength coach, standing in his office talking to another player. Last spring, Coach Walker had invested time in coaching me up, when other coaches could have thought, *This kid's not going to make the team anyway; why bother working with him?*

I stepped into his office. "Hey, Coach."

He looked at me for a second, puzzled. I could tell he recognized me but couldn't quite reconcile the guy standing before him with the 185-pound, not-as-muscular guy he saw last April. Instead of saying hi to me, he turned to the other player in his office and asked, "What's your excuse?"

I laughed and turned to leave. It felt good that he noticed the change. He could tell I had put in some serious work during the off-season. As I joined the guys for the first workout of the new year, I wondered if it would be enough.

THE TRYOUT: ROUND 2

After Coach T had given me the okay to try out again in December, I ramped up my running to shed some weight and increase my speed. I knew that no matter how much stronger or bigger I got, if I couldn't run, I wasn't going to make the team, and I needed to be in the best shape possible for mat drills. By the time tryouts rolled around, I had trimmed down to 220.

Like the previous year, we spent January in the weight room. There were even more people trying out than the year before. On our first day, Coach T had everyone max out on squats. I had a specific number in mind. When it was my turn, I loaded the bar with four plates on each side, totaling 405. That was more than I'd ever done. I figured if I could start the tryout off with that, I would make a statement.

I walked up to the rack and bent my legs slightly, letting the bar rest across my shoulders. I took a deep breath, straightened my legs, and lifted the weight off the rack. It felt heavy enough to crush my spine. I let my body sink down so that my quads were parallel with the floor. Then I stood up slowly, straining to straighten my legs.

Once I was standing upright, I racked the bar and then stepped back, trying to catch my breath. I felt Winston patting me on the back and congratulating me, but I couldn't really hear what he was saying because my ears were ringing. I had achieved a new personal best on my first attempt.

In the last week of January, we had a testing day on bench press and the forty-yard dash. Most of the scholarship players at my position could bench-press 225 pounds fifteen to twenty times. Last January I had benched it one time, but this year, I did twelve. I still didn't quite match the other linebackers, but I had closed the gap. They were no longer a whole world stronger than me.

The last time I had been tested at the forty-yard dash was in my senior year in high school, when I ran it in 5.6 seconds. That January, I ran a 5.0 while weighing seventy-five pounds more than I had in high school. My dedication to speed workouts had paid off. Now I knew my body could handle my current weight while running faster than I ever had before. Craig was in my testing group as well. In his first workout after shoulder surgery the previous fall, he set a team record, becoming the first player to rank in the top ten in both forty time and 225 bench reps since the current strength staff had started measuring those stats. Players are usually exceptionally fast or strong, not both, and especially not on the first day back in action.

In February, we moved into mat drills. On the first day, I set my alarm for 2:00 a.m. instead of the usual 3:45 and watched *Rocky II* before heading over, just to get myself in the zone.

When I got to the football facility that morning, I ran into Craig.

"You ready for this?" he asked me.

"Oh, yeah. I've been up since two. I watched *Rocky II* to get focused," I answered.

"No way! That's what I did. Exact same movie." We laughed. While everyone else was dragging themselves in, half asleep, we were wide awake and ready to go.

Mat drills proceeded the same as they had the year before. I felt more prepared because I knew what was coming, but I also knew it would still be a challenge to make the team. To set myself apart, I gave extra effort every chance I got. At the mat station, for example, I sprinted back to the start even when my group got a thumbs-up. The coaches didn't mind if we walked back after a thumbs-up, but I figured sprinting would show there was no way they were going to break me.

Some of the guys in my group didn't like the fact that I sprinted back after a thumbs-up, but I didn't care. I was too focused on doing the absolute best I could. One time when I sprinted back, Mike Bobo, the offensive coordinator, saw me and called out, "Now *there* is someone who wants to play football for Georgia!" And that's exactly what I wanted to show: I wasn't there to get a thumbs-up and then slow down and catch my breath. I really wanted to be part of this program.

After mat drills, we moved into spring practice. I felt more confident than the year before. Each drill was easier because I'd already been through it. I knew what to expect.

Coaches don't invest a lot of time teaching the playbook to guys trying out unless they later make the team; you just have to learn it on your own. Knowing the plays from last year helped a lot. One drill the team did in practice was pass skeleton. The offense had a quarterback and five guys playing receiver, tight end, or running back, and the defense had a total of seven guys in coverage. Every play was a pass.

This was an important drill for me to make an impression. I had already showed improvement in strength, speed, and fitness. Now I needed to show those skills translated onto the football field.

Coaches rotated the majority of the guys in and out of this drill, so I had several opportunities to play. The irony is that if you're doing a good job on defense, the ball doesn't get thrown your way, so you don't have an opportunity to make a play. When I rotated in, I usually got three plays per practice, which isn't a lot, but I wanted to make sure I was executing while I was in there.

Spring practice during my sophomore year, March 2009.

Almost every time I got in, I was assigned to cover my friend Craig in the slot; it just worked out that way when we stayed in our base defense instead of bringing in an extra cornerback. At any level of football, when a linebacker is covering a wide receiver, it's a mismatch in favor of the offense. My matchup with Craig was no exception— he was much faster than me.

In the first few days of this matchup, nothing happened one way or another; no passes were thrown his way, so I didn't have a chance to defend. A few times he was fairly open, but the quarterback threw to someone else. Finally, in the second week, I dropped back to cover the hook, a zone about ten yards deep. Craig lined up at slot receiver on my side and ran a slant route. The quarterback threw a quick pass, which bounced off Craig's hands and flew out to the side. I snagged it out of the air for an interception and ran about fifteen yards until someone on offense tagged me. Winston was playing cornerback and came over to celebrate after the play.

A week later, I lined up opposite another slot receiver, who beat me on the route, caught the ball, and started running. I chased him, and when he juked to avoid the safety, he slowed up enough for me to catch up and punch the ball. It flew right out of his arms into the safety's hands.

In the fifteen or so plays I was in pass skeleton that spring, the ball came my way twice, and both times I forced turnovers. I was really happy about those results. The first year, I didn't even get to participate in this drill. This year, I wasn't just in the drill; I was making plays.

Coaches rotated players in groups by their position in the depth chart; for example, the ones would go in, then the twos, and so on. My group was the fours, but I wasn't really fourth string. There were probably six or seven strings, and they rotated all the lower groups with the fours because they didn't want to rotate through seven groups. As a result, I didn't get into many drills, because there were a lot of guys rotating into the fours group.

G-DAY

During spring scrimmages, coaches graded players on every play using a simple plus/minus system: either you did your job according to the play call or you didn't. If you graded out at 70 percent or higher, you were doing well. We had three scrimmages before the spring game. After each one, coaches posted our scores, and I was consistently grading out higher on my performance than I had the year before. I really started to see myself having a spot on the team.

Then came the spring game. I was on the red team, and Winston and Craig were both on black. My parents and sisters attended, just like they had the year before.

I had a sense of urgency about this game. I knew it was my last chance to make an impression on my position coach. I didn't know how many plays I would be in the game, but

I had to make the most of them. I really wanted to put an exclamation point on a good tryout and show the coaches I could be an asset to this team.

The game was a defensive battle, and the first half ended in a 3–3 tie. At the end of the third quarter, the game was still tied, and I hadn't seen any playing time yet. Near the end of the fourth quarter, I started pacing the sidelines, worried I wouldn't get into the game. Even though it was a scrimmage, I wondered if coaches would put in guys who were trying out when the game was so close.

The red team made a field goal to go up 6–3. Shortly after, Coach Jancek called my name and a couple of others to let us know we were going in. I was excited to go in at such an important point in the game.

Our job on defense was to stop the black team's two-minute drill and hold on for the win. On first down, the offense ran the ball up the middle. Then they threw a pass and picked up some yards, and on the third play they got a first down. At that point, the coaches switched everyone out. They brought in some second-string guys to finish the drive, and they stopped the black team from scoring. When the red team offense came back out, they scored a touchdown on the last play of the game to win 13–3.

When we took the bus back to Butts-Mehre, I headed

straight for the linebacker meeting room to watch film of the game. Charles White and Akeem Hebron were already there turning on the projector. I sat and reviewed each play I was involved in, thinking through what I could have done better. I didn't make any mistakes, but I didn't make any plays either. I tried to see it from my position coach's perspective: had I done enough for him to argue for me to make the team instead of the other guys trying out? There was only one way to find out, and it was happening soon.

DECISION TIME: ROUND 2

A week after the spring game, I walked into the linebacker coach's office for what I thought was a performance-review meeting.

"Hi, Candler. Have a seat," Coach Jancek said, looking up from what he was reading.

After I sat down, he continued. "So, we've gone through the roster and the openings we have, and we've decided who we have room for and, unfortunately, we don't have room for you at this time."

His words completely caught me off guard. I expected to find out where I had done well, what I still needed to work on, and so on. I didn't know they had already made roster decisions. It didn't happen this way the year before.

When I didn't answer right away, Coach Jancek continued. "I can tell that you have improved a lot, Candler. Would you be interested in playing football at another school?"

"No," I replied without hesitation. "I came to Georgia because this is where I want to play football."

"Okay."

At that point there wasn't much left to say, so I thanked him for the opportunity to try out, got up, and left his office.

I headed straight to the locker room, feeling empty and disappointed. I opened my locker and took out my cleats and clothes. I had to remove all signs of myself so someone who had made the team could use the space. I reached up to the top shelf to make sure I hadn't missed anything and found a single sheet of paper. It was a review sheet completed by Coach T. There were several categories on the top half of the page—speed, strength, pass defense, run defense—but coaches only fill these out if you make the team. Coach T wrote the following at the bottom of the page, including the misspelled name:

Chandler has made great progress over the last year. He transformed his body. I appreciate his commitment and work ethic. However, he leveled off in his development... His body could not handle any more weight; his strength leveled off. His speed got worse because he's as big as he can get, and for him it's too big...He does not have the fast-twitch muscle needed to play in SEC...too small, too slow, not quick...average strength. I appreciate his want, desire, and effort, but he must face facts. He is a Division III football player at best and should strongly consider giving it up.

I felt like I'd been punched in the stomach. I reread the letter slowly, taking a minute to let it soak in.

By this point, other players had finished meeting with their position coaches and read their own letters after they cleaned out their lockers. It was quiet for a few minutes before the guy in the locker next to me asked, "What did yours say?"

I handed him the letter. When he finished reading, he handed it back and said, "Dude, that's harsh."

I put on my headphones and left the locker room. Last time I had been cut, Brian was with me, and we were able to talk things through. This time, I was all alone. I felt numb. I just started walking while blaring heavy-metal music on my iPod. A million thoughts raced through my mind as I tried to process the gravity of what had just happened. I really thought I was close to making the team. As I walked, I turned up the music louder and louder.

I walked straight down Sanford Drive, the street that runs from the practice facility to the stadium. I walked across the bridge that overlooks the west end zone—the same one I'd stood on with my dad before games years earlier. It was late afternoon on a weekday, and the stadium was quiet. I stared out over the field: the place I wanted to be was right there, and yet it seemed so far away. There could not be 125 people in the world who wanted to be on that field as badly as I did. There just couldn't.

I stood there for ten minutes, lost in thought. Giving up was not an option. I would not let those comments dissuade me. I was determined to try out every single year until I ran out of eligibility.

I walked back to my dorm to figure out my next steps. I lived with Brian at the time and showed him the comment sheet. He was as shocked as I was. Finally, I took the paper and walked into my room. "Are you going to shred that?" Brian asked me.

"No. I'm making copies."

YOUR TURN

Pursuing a goal is like one big mat drill. After chopping your feet, moving back and forth, hitting the mat, and jumping back up, then chopping your feet again and racing through the finish line, you wait for the coach's decision: thumbs-up or thumbs-down.

If your goal is big enough, you are almost certainly going to get a thumbs-down at some point. When that happens, you can respond in one of two ways: you can feel sorry for yourself and maybe even give up, or you can keep going. If you're going to reach an impossible goal, you can't let rejection define or deter you. You have to pick yourself up and look for the next opportunity to succeed.

Sometimes you can get caught up in one moment on the way to achieving your goal. You might think that as soon as you accomplish that one thing, success will be just around the corner. And then it's not.

I thought I had done enough to make the team—all those extra meals, extra workouts, extra running drills, and extra effort. I had definitely improved; the coaches told me that, and my accomplishments in the gym showed me that. But I still didn't make the team.

I could have crumbled after reading that comment sheet—a major personal thumbs-down—but I chose to stay positive. No matter what was written on that page, I was still in full control of my life. What a tragedy it would have been if I had let those words determine my destiny.

Have you experienced rejection despite giving everything you have, when it seemed as if you were almost there? How did you respond?

CHAPTER 6

REINVENTING MYSELF

The last three or four reps is what makes the muscle grow. This area of pain divides a champion from someone who is not a champion. That's what most people lack. Having the guts to go on and just say they'll go through the pain no matter what happens.

—ARNOLD SCHWARZENEGGER, *PUMPING IRON*

Final exams started a few weeks after I got cut. Given my current meal schedule, I couldn't go three hours without eating, so I came prepared.

I took a seat and unzipped my backpack. The class was quiet except for the shuffling of paper as students scanned their notes one last time. Instead of reviewing, I took out a Tupperware container, cracked the lid, and pulled out my snack. I bit into it and then glanced to my right. The girl next to me was staring, horrified.

"Is that a potato?" she asked.

I nodded and kept chewing. She shuddered and went back to her notes.

During the exam, I ate two plain baked potatoes and drank a protein shake. I guess eating a potato like it was an apple did look a little odd. I had a goal, and a final exam wasn't going to get in the way. I didn't really care what other people thought.

MOTIVATION

After making copies of my review sheet, I left them all over my dorm room: on the refrigerator, on the bathroom counter, and on the bedside table. I wanted to internalize the evaluation and use it as motivation to improve to the point where I couldn't be denied a spot on the team. From that moment on, whenever I was running or working out, the words *too small, too slow, average strength* ran through my head. The final remark about giving it up implied that my goal was impossible and that there was no way I would ever play football at Georgia. The problem with that suggestion is that I'm in charge of creating my own destiny, so I decide what is impossible for myself.

Around this time, I started hearing negative, snarky comments from people at the gym, other guys who had tried out with me, and random people who went to high schools in my hometown. On Facebook and to my face, people made comments like "How many times are you going to keep getting cut? Don't you hold the record already?" I didn't bother responding, but it surprised me that people would take time to drag others down. Maybe they wanted to see others fail since they couldn't achieve their own dreams. At the same time, their opinions really didn't matter to me. I was too focused on my goal—on putting one foot in front of the other and making sure I was doing the best I could every single day—to let things like that bother me.

A key part of my journey was being steady in my thoughts and emotions. A great attitude can turn around even the bleakest of situations, and a poor attitude can ruin excellent opportunities. When negative things happened to me, I never allowed them to bother me or cause me to give up, because negativity does not exist in my world—there is upbeat and positive, and nothing else. Guys who were much better football players than I was never made the team, because they could not overcome setbacks and stay positive. I was committed to making sure that nothing would knock me off my path. As an African proverb says, "When there is no enemy within, the enemies outside cannot hurt you."

RIDICULOUS NEW MEASURES

By getting cut as a sophomore, I would not be on the team the fall of my junior year. The next time I could possibly try out would be the following spring. I could redshirt once, but even including a redshirt year, I only had two seasons left to play. I was on my next-to-last chance to make the team before I ran out of eligibility.

I needed to find a way to reinvent myself. I was already working out nonstop, running more than most guys, and eating eight meals a day. I made it through mat drills and gave my all every single practice. Still, it was not enough. I couldn't keep trying harder at the same plan; I needed to do something completely different. My ridiculous goal required ridiculous measures.

NEW EATING SCHEDULE

An important part of my new plan involved shifting to ten meals a day. I knew there was no way I'd make the team at my current size; I had to get bigger. Eight meals had worked for a while, but I had plateaued, so I needed to bump it up. I started this step the day after I got cut in April.

Within a few days, I could tell I couldn't eat that much without getting physically sick. I wasn't a professional eater, and my stomach could only hold so much food.

From bodybuilding websites such as Animal Pak, I learned that whole milk was an excellent way to get calories without eating solid food, so I added it to my nutrition plan—two gallons per day. Animal Pak also provided ideas for keeping meals enjoyable and interesting—like adding Splenda to oatmeal and including shakes with bananas, peanut butter, and protein powder at some meals.

If you make a big play in a football game, the crowd goes crazy. If you make a big lift in the gym, your friends congratulate you and random people might stop to watch. When you eat an incredible amount of food to get bigger, however, nobody else cares. You must be disciplined and completely self-driven. Eating right is the most important part of gaining muscle, and it's also the most overlooked. I knew a lot of people who worked hard in the gym or at practice but never saw results, because doing the right things one hour a day in the weight room doesn't make up for a bad diet and poor choices in the remaining twenty-three hours.

Because I didn't know anyone else who was on this kind of eating plan, I went online for inspiration. I watched videos on the YouTube channel Muscle Prodigy, and one in particular really helped me through the eating regimen. In the video, called "Motivation for Life," Jaret Grossman talks about the importance of every aspect of a training plan, even when you don't get recognition for it:

You don't set out to build a wall. Instead you say, "I'm going to lay this brick as perfectly as a brick can be laid." You do that every single day, and soon enough you have a wall...In order to get a thousand, you need a thousand ones. Now each one seems insignificant, but you need every one of those to add up to a thousand.

This perfectly summarized my mentality: every day, every workout, and every meal was like a brick I was putting in place to build a wall. Every brick brought me one small step closer to my goal.

The menu I followed on a typical ten-meal day looked like this:

- 7:15 a.m.: four eggs (scrambled, fried, or an omelet), two cups of oatmeal, thirty-two ounces of whole milk
- 9:30 a.m.: three egg whites, two sausage patties, two cups of grits, thirty-two ounces of whole milk
- 11:00 a.m.: two ten-ounce steaks, three sweet potatoes, one cup of spinach, thirty-two ounces of whole milk
- 12:30 p.m.: eight ounces of grilled chicken, two cups of white rice, a cup of cantaloupe, three ten-ounce peanut butter and banana smoothies
- 2:00 p.m.: two peanut butter and jelly sandwiches, three sweet potatoes, thirty-two ounces of whole milk
- 3:30 p.m.: two turkey sandwiches, one banana, thirty-two ounces of whole milk

- 5:30 p.m.: one ten-ounce steak, three sweet potatoes, Caesar salad, three ten-ounce peanut butter and banana smoothies
- 7:00 p.m.: eight ounces of grilled fish (usually tilapia or grouper), two cups of white rice, one cup of watermelon, thirty-two ounces of whole milk
- 8:30 p.m.: one beef and cheese burrito with salsa and lettuce, three sweet potatoes, one cup of spinach, thirty-two ounces of whole milk
- 10:00 p.m.: four egg whites, one bagel with cream cheese, thirty-two ounces of whole milk

I put this nutrition plan together on my own, based on my class and workout schedule and information I'd read online. In whole milk alone, I consumed about forty-eight hundred calories a day; in total, I was taking in at least fifteen thousand calories. I also drank at least three gallons of water a day. If you're eating that much food, you really need to stay hydrated, especially if you're working out as much as I was.

I had to change my class schedule because of my new eating plan. Starting the fall of my junior year, I scheduled classes so that I never had two in a row. I always had a class, then a break, then a class, and so on. I had to make time to eat before and after every single class.

NEW TRAINING PLAN

As part of my new workout plan, I needed a new work-out partner—someone who would really challenge me while I was home in Atlanta for the summer. I remembered that Craig had told me about a "freakishly strong" friend named Jarrett Moore who went to Kennesaw State and was studying exercise physiology. I figured he would be the perfect person to train with. I contacted Jarrett, and he agreed.

The first day we worked out together, I weighed 218; that was my baseline for the summer. I reinstated my goal of gaining two pounds a week.

Jarrett and I set up a routine training four days a week at either Kennesaw State or Coffee's Gym in Marietta, Georgia. We would lift weights for an hour and then do fifteen minutes of sprints or agility drills at the end.

Jarrett introduced me to exercises I had never even heard of. On legs day, for example, we would start with normal squats. Then when our legs were already tired, we would do hack squats—using a machine where the weight rests on your shoulders and you push yourself up and back at an angle, almost like a rocket ship taking off. We also did split squat dumbbell lunges: you hold a dumbbell in each hand and stand with your legs staggered, back foot resting on a bench; then you dip straight down until your back knee almost touches the floor. When Jarrett and I trained legs, it usually took five days for my legs to recover and stop being sore—just in time for another legs day.

After each workout, Jarrett and I immediately ate together. When I got home, I ate again. I started seeing results by the end of my first week. Pretty soon, I was able to bench 315 for the first time.

Working out with someone stronger than me pushed me to work harder—and Jarrett was significantly stronger. Whereas I was able to squat 405, he could squat 600. Jarrett was polite and friendly outside the gym, but when it was time to train, he had an intense, fiery focus. Working out with him was inspiring.

While I was training in Atlanta, the team was working out in Athens. Several times during workouts I thought, *There's no way on earth they're doing this kind of workout.* I knew I was out-training all of them.

Toward the end of that summer, I went on a vacation with my family. I needed to stay on my training routine, so I looked up gyms in the area and found a local YMCA two blocks from where we were staying. On the first day, I walked over to check out the equipment and lift. It was back day, which was my favorite.

The gym was empty when I arrived. I put on my iPod and started blaring Five Finger Death Punch, one of my favorite heavy-metal bands. I loaded the bar for dead lifts and then realized I had left my chalk at home in Atlanta. When I lifted that much weight, I used chalk so the bar wouldn't slip out of my hands. *Oh, well*, I thought. *I'll just do what I can without it.*

With each set, I loaded more weight on the bar. I could feel my grip slipping a little more every time. For my last set, I decided to try 500 pounds for a set of three. Previously, I had only lifted that much for a single rep. I loaded the plates on both ends and stared at the bar for a second before lifting it. The bar started to slip as I stood up, but I was able to hold it. I gathered myself and did a second rep, then a third, both times barely hanging on to the bar. When I set the bar down for the third time, I heard a noise behind me. I turned and saw a middle-aged man sitting at a machine in the corner.

"Oh my gosh," he said. "I've never seen someone lift that much weight in my entire life."

I paused for a moment. It never occurred to me that now I was strong by most people's standards. I still saw myself as the little kid from high school.

By the end of summer, I had gained twenty-four pounds,

keeping up with my goal of gaining two pounds per week. I was up to 242, a new all-time high. In August, I headed back to Athens, knowing I still had five months until I could try out again.

NEW MINDSET

Early in the fall semester of my junior year, I had a terrible dream: as in reality, I had tried out for the football team, was cut after spring practice, and then worked out over the fall and winter to prepare for the next tryout. But this time, when I approached Coach T about trying out, he said, "No, we actually meant you can't try out again."

I woke with a start. My forehead and arms were drenched in sweat. I was breathing heavily, and it took me a few seconds to realize I was in my dorm room and it was just a dream. It really shook me.

I looked at the clock: 3:15 a.m. I knew I couldn't go back to sleep, so I got up and threw on a T-shirt, shorts, and shoes. I lived on the sixth floor of the dorm. I walked down to the first floor, turned around, and sprinted up the stairs—all six flights. When I got to the top, I turned around and headed back down. At the bottom, I turned and sprinted back up. Then back down. Then back up. Then back down. I lost count of how many trips I made. Every time I wanted to stop, I told myself, *One more rep.*

That's the one that's going to get me on the football team. My legs burned with each flight I climbed, but I ignored the feeling and kept going.

I wasn't watching the time, so I have no idea how long I continued, but eventually my body stopped feeling tired. In that moment, I knew what the few guys who dominated mat drills felt like. In that moment, I knew my mind had finally won the battle over my body. In that moment, I knew I could keep going up and down those stairs forever.

After my last trip down the stairs, I continued running out of the building. I hustled across the quad with the wind whipping around me, past some academic buildings, and into the twenty-four-hour dining hall. When I walked into the building at 4:30 a.m., dripping with sweat, I got a few funny looks from the staff. I ordered a five-egg omelet, loaded up three cups of oatmeal, and took a seat. As I ate, I reflected on what just happened. I knew I had turned a corner: I had just discovered what it meant to truly give my all and not let pain or fatigue prevent me from achieving what I wanted.

NEW GOALS

In my junior year, I felt a sense of urgency I hadn't experienced before. This was now the third season of football without me being on the team. Time was running out, and I had a lot of work to do.

That fall, I set up a new workout routine, largely training by myself using the student gym. I focused on tackling the weight-lifting goals Craig and I had come up with:

- power clean 300 pounds
- bench-press 400 pounds
- squat 500 pounds
- deadlift 600 pounds

One afternoon, Craig and I were hanging out. We had just eaten, watched *Rocky IV*, eaten again, and then headed to the weight room.

When we walked in, I weighed myself: 245. I had officially gained one hundred pounds since I'd started college two years earlier. I went through my deadlift warm-up routine, starting with one plate on each side of the bar, then two plates, and so on, until I reached my goal.

After loading the plates, I chalked up my hands and stood over the bar for a second, readying myself. I kept thinking of the words on that evaluation sheet—*too small, too slow, average strength*. My hands started shaking and my skin turned white hot. *Too small, too slow, average strength.* I stepped up to the bar, bent down, and put my hands on it. It was just me and the bar, no straps or belts. *Too small, too slow, average strength.* I started pulling as hard as I could. I felt the weight ever-so-slowly break contact with the floor; inch by inch I raised the bar. *Too small, too slow, average strength.* Every muscle in my body was shaking, but I held tight and kept standing up until—finally—I locked it out. I stood there for a second. Then I let go of the bar, and it thudded to the ground. I had just deadlifted 600 pounds, a number I had never seen anyone on the Georgia football team do. If I could do that, why in the world couldn't I make that team?

NEW POSITION

My final change was to reevaluate my position on the field.

I knew my strengths and weaknesses: I had become a lot stronger, but I was still very slow compared to other guys playing linebacker. I had never been a quick-burst type of athlete; I was more of an endurance athlete. The closer you play to the line of scrimmage, the slower you can be. You still need some quickness getting off the line, but you don't need to be as fast as someone playing linebacker.

Given these facts, I made a risky, unconventional move: I decided to switch from linebacker to defensive end, a position I had never played at any level, not even youth league.

In my mind, switching positions gave me the best chance to make the team. There were more 220-pound, athletic walk-ons than 250-pound, athletic walk-ons. This meant less competition. Plus, even though I had never actually played defensive end, the position helped mask my speed deficiency.

At the end of the regular season, Georgia fired three of the defensive coaches. The only defensive coach Georgia kept was Rodney Garner, the defensive line coach and assistant head coach. Then the team hired Todd Grantham as the new defensive coordinator. He announced they would be changing the defense to a 3-4 instead of a 4-3. In other words, we would now have three defensive linemen and four linebackers, which is more of an NFL-style defense.

I looked up what this change meant for defensive ends and discovered it required bigger, stronger players but not as much speed. A 4-3 defensive end is mostly focused on holding his own against the run and also being a good edge rusher on pass plays, whereas a 3-4 defensive end is mostly concerned with taking on double teams on run plays and with pass rush on the inside. On the whole, the shift to a 3-4 defense seemed as if it would work in my favor and further thin out the competition at defensive end.

Most of the scholarship guys who played defensive end in

a 3-4 weighed 280 to 300 pounds—a lot bigger than the guys who play in a 4-3, who were around 260. Walk-ons could be smaller than the scholarship players, but not by too much. That meant I still had some work to do in the weight-gain department.

I realized there might be one other factor that could work to my advantage: since three of the four defensive coaches were new to the program, it was possible that no one would recognize me. They might not realize I'd tried out twice before at a different position, so they wouldn't have any preconceived notions to judge me by.

After I decided that I wanted to play defensive end, I taught myself the position by watching YouTube videos. I spent hours watching highlights of NFL defensive ends who were doing well. I looked at their stance, how they reacted to different plays, techniques they used, and so on. I watched how they were able to get off blocks and take on double teams. Then I went to the practice field and tried to emulate their moves. Sometimes I practiced with Craig, but he was on the team and had fall practices and games. Most of the time, I was out there by myself, getting in a stance, responding as if the ball was hiked and I was taking on offensive linemen. There was no one out there to critique me, but I just tried to keep in mind the images of what the NFL players had done. I also set up cones and ran agility drills and pass rush drills. I ran around the cones to get to an imaginary quarterback—the football dummy I had set up. I weaved in and out of bags, hoping to get the hang of things before doing those drills in front of a coach. Trying out for a new position was an uncertain move, but it was also the kind of outside-the-box thinking needed to achieve my goal.

NEW ATTITUDE

At the end of fall semester, I walked into Coach T's office once again. The door was open, but I knocked lightly to get his attention.

"Yes?" Coach T asked.

I stepped inside. "I want to try out for the football team."

He looked at me and said, "Okay."

"See you in January," I replied, and then turned around and walked out. That was it. I didn't ask. I didn't mention last spring or the review sheet. I just told him what I wanted.

As I walked back toward my dorm, I thought, *If I can gain a hundred pounds and deadlift 600, I can play football for Georgia.* I knew it. I had proved to myself that I belonged; now I just needed to show everyone else.

YOUR TURN

In the movie *The Dark Knight Rises*, Batman tries to escape from prison by scaling a wall with only a rope around his waist to keep him from plunging to his death. After the second unsuccessful attempt, an elderly man tells him, "You do not fear death. You think this makes you strong. It makes you weak. How can you move faster than possible, fight longer than possible, without the most powerful impulse of the spirit: the fear of death? Make the climb without the rope. Then fear will find you again." After that, Batman climbs the giant wall and makes a ridiculous jump without the rope, knowing that if he misses, he will die.

As I approached preparation for my third tryout, I had the same mindset: I had to give my all and make the ridiculous jump without a rope—eating more, working out harder, changing positions—not knowing if it was going to work. I also had to acknowledge that I was afraid: afraid of having to live with that empty feeling of cleaning out my locker, afraid of letting myself down, and most of all, afraid of dying one day without ever having played in a Georgia football game.

To reach my goal, I had to be willing to try something completely different; I couldn't just try harder. Doing the same thing with more intensity or effort works sometimes, but other times it's not enough. When that happens, you have to be willing to step back and reevaluate your approach. You might need to reinvent yourself, your methods, or your plan of attack. The new plan might look crazy to other people. That's okay. You have to be willing to dive in and go for it, even though there's no guarantee it will work. Are you stuck in pursuit of your goal? Have you considered a different approach, style, or method? Research different options and learn as much as you can. It may be the key to overcoming the trickiest of obstacles.

CHAPTER 7

BREAKTHROUGH

That which we attain too easily, we esteem too lightly.

—THOMAS PAINE

In the first week of January 2010, I walked into the health center for my pre-tryout physical. I asked for the same doctor who had done the physical the last two years and took a seat in the waiting room.

"Candler Cook?" the nurse called from the doorway.

I got up and followed her to the scale. I stepped on and watched her move the sliders right and left, trying to get the needle to balance. She noted my weight and wrote the number down on my chart. Then her eyes narrowed for a second and darted back and forth between the number she had just written down and something at the top of the page. She paused, looked up at me, and said, "Wait here for just a second." She walked into the back room.

I stepped off the scale and smiled. I knew what she was thinking—that she had the wrong chart. The number in the weight column from two years ago said 145; the scale had just showed 250.

About two minutes later, the nurse returned. "So, we're doing random steroid testing, and you've been selected," she said, handing me a cup.

"Okay," I said and took the cup. I laughed to myself and thought, *Doesn't seem random to me.* I took care of business and left the office. I wasn't worried about the result; I knew the reason for my radical change.

Now there was no denying that I had completely transformed my body. If the doctors didn't recognize me, maybe the coaches wouldn't, either. I could approach this tryout as a completely different person trying out for a new position and hopefully have a different outcome.

THE TRYOUT: ROUND 3

During the initial tryout meeting, we filled out forms with basic information, including what position we wanted to try out for. This time, instead of linebacker, I wrote in defensive end.

As a result of my new position, January workouts took place with a new group of guys—the linemen—who were even bigger and stronger than the big skill group I had worked out with the previous two years. These guys were huge; several weighed well over three hundred pounds. Because of this, I had a much easier time keeping up during sprints. Now I was running with the slowest position group on the team, so I didn't stick out in a bad way like I did before.

In the weight room, I wasn't just stronger; I had a different attitude as well, and the other guys could see it. I was trying to be more of a leader. While some guys were going through the motions and not lifting as much as they could or completing all of their reps, I was going all out every time. I would strain to lift as much as I could at each station and then sprint to the next machine. My enthusiasm and energy were so high and constant that some of the guys started calling me Lattimer, an intense character from the football movie *The Program*.

During the first two months of tryouts, I also spent more time watching YouTube videos and working on technique. Spring practice was just around the corner, and I wanted to get as familiar with defensive end techniques as possible so I would know what to do once practice started.

At the first scrimmage, the coaches had four plays set aside for the third-string guys to run. Due to the shortage of guys who could play defensive end in a 3-4, I was third string now. I went over the plays in my head and waited for my turn.

Toward the end of the day, Coach Garner called for the third stringers to take the field. I ran out to the huddle and listened to the play call, making sure I had my assignment right. I lined up in a five technique, which is on the outside shoulder of the offensive tackle. My responsibility was to shoot inside him and cover the B gap between the guard and the tackle.

The quarterback took the snap from the center and handed it off to the running back. I moved to take over the gap. The running back headed away from me at first, and then tried to cut back across the middle toward my side. I moved inside and stopped him right at the line of scrimmage by myself. The second stringers came in a few plays later, but I was happy to have made a play on just four snaps.

Each day while the skill and big skill groups were doing pass skeleton, the linemen did one-on-one pass rush.

Because of the nature of the drill, all eyes were on the two people facing off. Toward the end of spring practice, I started getting a turn at the end of the drill. On the second day, I had my first win, using a rip move to get around a 285-pound offensive lineman. I ran back to the line and heard a few guys encouraging me. My technique was still choppy and unrefined, but I felt like I was getting more comfortable with this new position.

Going one-on-one in a drill against six-foot-six, 365-pound Kwame Geathers during spring practice in my third tryout, March 2010. At this point I had gained more than one hundred pounds since I'd started college.

DECISION TIME: ROUND 3

When the spring game came around, I was on the red team again. I got in for eight plays, although I didn't make any tackles. After the spring game, we had two weeks of workouts while coaches decided who would make the team. Then we set up a meeting with our position coach. *The* meeting. The one where I would learn whether all my ridiculous measures had been enough.

On the day of my meeting with Coach Garner, I headed to his office on the second floor of the football building. The door was open. I looked in and saw him sitting at his desk. He noticed me and said, "Come in."

I took a seat opposite the desk, just like I had done last year in a different office with a different position coach.

"Candler, you've done well this spring," Coach started, looking down at his notes. "You also have some areas to work on. You need to improve your pass rush skills. We're looking for a quick burst off the line of scrimmage." He spent the next ten minutes going into specific skills for my position, and then he said, "I think there's a place for you on this team. You need to get bigger and stronger this summer so you can help out on the scout team and run the other team's plays in practice this fall."

My heart stopped for a second. I couldn't hear anything

while I tried to comprehend what he had just said. The rest of the meeting could have been one minute or twenty; I was in shock, so I couldn't tell.

I guess I had always imagined balloons and streamers would shoot down from the ceiling when I heard this news, but Coach Garner was matter-of-fact, as if from the beginning he had fully expected me to make the team.

"Here's the workout book to follow this summer," he said, handing me a three-ring binder. I stood to take it.

"Thank you," I said, and then left his office.

I walked downstairs. It was so surreal. For the longest time, it seemed like this moment would never actually happen, and now it had. I opened the locker-room doors—the same ones I'd walked through a hundred times. Everything felt different. For the first time, this was *my* locker room. I wasn't an outsider anymore. I wouldn't be sharing a locker with someone. I would be practicing year-round instead of just in the spring, and I'd get my very own jersey with my name on the back. I might even be able to dress out and play in a game. The thing I had spent so many years striving for was finally mine. I was a Georgia Bulldog. My life had just changed forever.

INSPIRATION

School finished for the year a few weeks later, and I went home to Atlanta for the rest of May and worked out with Jarrett again.

He took me to the North Georgia Barbell gym in Kennesaw—one of the most intense gyms I have ever been to. Nearly every guy in there weighed at least three hundred pounds and warmed up with weight heavier than my max. I watched a girl squat 500, which is more than many college football players can do.

Among the guys working out, I spotted an older man named Tom Sisk who was lifting like someone half his age. I learned he was seventy-five years old. Three years earlier he had been diagnosed with cancer and was given a few months to live. At the time he had been out of shape, but one of his life goals was to be a powerlifter, even though he had never tried it before. After being diagnosed with cancer, he decided to chase down that goal. After three years of training and beating cancer, he was now the bench-press world-record holder for his age group and weight class.

Here was a guy who had every excuse to give up and think it was too late to go after his goal: old age, cancer diagnosis, and being out of shape. But he didn't. He started where he was and took it one step at a time until he became the world record holder. I could identify with this guy. He had overcome much worse odds than I had faced, and he had made it.

FIRST SUMMER WORKOUTS

When I returned to Athens in June, I had a surprise waiting for me: my own locker with my name on it. It was such a cool sight.

The team followed the workout book I'd been given and added a day of strongman work—unconventional weight training you might see in World's Strongest Man competitions. We pounded tires with sledgehammers, pushed sleds, and flipped tires. We did farmer's walks, where we'd pick up hundred-pound dumbbells in each hand and walk as far as we could. Plus, we were doing these drills at two in the afternoon in hundred-degree weather. We were on AstroTurf, with a concrete wall right next to us, reflecting the sun back onto the field. It was brutal.

At the end of summer, we did a conditioning test where we ran sixteen 110-yard sprints on the field with about thirty seconds between each one. Each group had to make a different time. My group, the linemen, had to run each sprint in twenty seconds or less. If the whole group didn't make the time, we all had to start over. I didn't want to be the one who stuck out and failed. We trained for this challenge in the eight weeks leading up to it. By the time the test came, I had done it three or four times a week, eight weeks in a row. At the beginning of the summer it was pretty rough, but it got easier.

After the conditioning test, the coaches posted a list of 105 players going to camp. I was not on it. I really hadn't expected to be, but I was still a little disappointed that I had to miss two weeks of practice while the other guys kept going.

During those two weeks, I went back to Atlanta and trained with Jarrett at North Georgia Barbell. I set a new personal best in the squat, doing 405 for a set of five reps; a year and a half earlier, I had maxed out at 405 for the first time. The next week, I squatted 450 for two reps, another personal best.

FIRST FALL PRACTICES

After my two weeks in Atlanta, I returned to Athens for my fourth year of college. Academically, I was a senior, but as far as football was concerned, this would be my redshirt junior season and I would have one more year of eligibility. One more full season as a Georgia Bulldog. And I wouldn't have to go through tryouts again.

This was the first time I joined the team for fall practices, and each day felt more exciting than the last. Every practice brought us closer to the season, when I might get to dress out and stand on the sidelines. At this point, I hadn't suited up for an actual game in four years—since my senior year of high school.

During fall practices, walk-ons get a lot of reps because they're helping the first- and second-string players get ready for each opponent. When you're on the scout team, you're not expected to beat the starters, but you are expected to go hard and at least give them a look—a sense of what they might see during the game. Being on scout team was both challenging and fun because I was matched up against the best guys on the team.

On the scout team, I mostly played nose guard because that was where the team needed me to help out. Nose guards are the biggest players on the entire defense and take on double-team blocks almost every play. That meant I had two 330-pound guys blocking me at the same time. At this point I weighed 255, so holding my own against two of those linemen felt like trying to stop an eighteen-wheeler going sixty-five miles an hour.

Two weeks before our first game, we practiced in the morning and then got ready for fan day. As we headed back to the locker room, I saw an equipment manager put something in my locker. I paused and craned my neck to see what it was—a red home jersey with my name on it. I walked over and held it up for a second and thought of how many years I had waited and how much hard work had gone into earning that jersey. I had watched count-less players wear that red Georgia uniform, and now I had one of my own.

First picture day as part of the team, August 2010. I'm standing with Rodney Garner, my position coach.

A few minutes later, we loaded the buses and headed to the stadium to sign autographs for fans. I looked for the table for my position group. The line of fans seemed to wrap around the entire block; I could only imagine how many people were waiting for the running backs and quarterbacks. We stayed there for two hours, meeting fans and signing everything from posters to books to T-shirts. The season was right around the corner.

FIRST GAME

SEC regulations state that each team can only have eighty-five guys on the sidelines during home games. Eighty-five also happens to be the number of scholarship players on a team. This means there's usually no room for a walk-on to dress out for conference home games, unless it's someone who starts on special teams. For nonconference home games, teams can dress out as many players as they want, and they usually dress out around one hundred. For conference road games, the team can dress out sixty-five; that means twenty scholarship players have to sit at home. I was so excited to be on the team, but I still had a lot of work to do if I wanted to suit up for any games, and my chances of dressing out for a big SEC opponent were slim to none.

The week after fan day, we prepared for our final scrimmage and put together the game plan for our first opponent of the season: Louisiana-Lafayette. That Wednesday, we had a mock game in Sanford Stadium, the final game-like situation before the season officially started. I got in for a few plays, although I didn't record any tackles.

As I was leaving that scrimmage, it hit me: the next time anyone set foot on the field, it would be for our first game of the season. My first game as a member of the team. I had waited so long for the chance to suit up for a game, and now it was almost here.

With each subsequent practice, I mentally marked off another day on the calendar, but the days leading up to game day seemed to crawl by. I was really hoping I would get to dress out. Louisiana-Lafayette was a nonconference home game, which meant that the team had no limit on the number of players they could have on the sidelines.

On Wednesday, September 1, I woke up early and headed to class. I could barely sit still or concentrate on anything the professor was saying. Coaches were posting the dress list that afternoon, and I was dying to know if I was on it. Years of waiting had been condensed to just hours. After lunch, I caught the first bus over to Butts-Mehre and ran into the locker room. At the far end of the room, a small crowd had gathered around a piece of paper taped to the wall: the dress list. I pushed my way to the front and scanned the sheet for my name. It was there! I just stared at it for a few seconds while the reality sunk in. Then I walked away from the crowd and sat down by myself. My eyes started watering as the significance of my name on that piece of paper hit me: after all the times when it felt impossible, when it seemed as if I would never be one of those guys on the field, it was about to happen. I thought about the last few years and the words written on my last evaluation: too small, too slow, average strength. Well, here I was, clearly big, fast, and strong enough to be a Georgia Bulldog.

The morning of the Louisiana-Lafayette game, I got up

and ate breakfast by myself in the dining hall, listening to music and thinking about the game. As I finished eating, my phone lit up with a text from Craig: "Good luck today. I'm proud of you. Dressing out for this game is such an honor." Craig had retired from football the spring before due to two shoulder surgeries. I respected him for the way he battled injuries and fought to make the team, so receiving that text meant a lot.

After breakfast, I walked over to Butts-Mehre and saw tailgate tents, TVs, and fans getting excited about the new season. Two young boys wearing Georgia jerseys were throwing a football around like I had done so many years earlier.

I walked into the locker room and saw a helmet, game jersey, and pants laid out, along with a program for the game. The uniform looked almost too perfect to wear, like it belonged in a museum.

I sat there listening to my iPod, knowing I was about to walk into a stadium filled to capacity with the same fans I'd sat next to as a kid; all eyes would be on me and my teammates.

The night before home games, the team bought hotel rooms out of town for the first- and second-string players and then bused them to the stadium. The rest of us stayed in Athens, got dressed at the football practice building, and took a bus to the east side of the stadium, where we met the first and second stringers at the locker room. Inside, trainers were taping players' ankles and wrists, equipment managers were handing out gloves, and student assistants were passing out fruit, protein bars, and Powerade.

About an hour before kickoff, we headed onto the field for warm-ups. It was a full house. As usual, Phil Collins's "In the Air Tonight" was playing over the loudspeakers. Next, the team huddled at midfield and then split into position groups. I ran to the corner of the end zone where Coach Garner was leading defensive line drills. Every rep felt like a real game. The stadium got louder and louder as kickoff approached.

After that, Coach Richt met with the whole team in the locker room for a pregame talk. In the background I could hear the highlight video rolling and the voice of Georgia's announcer, Larry Munson. As we left the locker room, I again read the sign posted above the door: "Be worthy as you run upon this hallowed sod, for you dare to tread where champions have trod."

We gathered in the tunnel, ready to run onto the field. The band and the deafening roar of the crowd echoed all around us. Several players at the front started jumping up and down, edging toward the tunnel's opening. When the crowd caught sight of them, the cheering reached a fever pitch. At the coach's signal, we ran out of the tunnel and burst through the banner. I had never felt so alive in my entire life. The band was playing the same songs I'd heard since I was five, but they sounded so much more powerful because they were playing for us, the guys on the field.

The game started slowly, but we ended up cruising to a 55–7 win. Being on the sidelines was every bit as amazing as I thought it would be. I didn't get to play, but I soaked up the experience: the crowd, the energy, the action, and the fact that I was there, on the field. All those years of hard work had paid off. I still wanted to play, but it was exciting just to be on the team. Getting to play was the next part of my goal.

YOUR TURN

If you have worked, sweated, and sacrificed to reach a goal, you will greatly appreciate the accomplishment once you achieve it. For me, making the football team took years, and the full weight of what I'd finally done snuck up on me. I was so focused on the work it took to get there that when I saw my name on the dress list, it suddenly hit me: three days from now I would be dressing out. With that realization, I took time to reflect and really appreciate what I had done. I remembered all the meals alone, strenuous workouts, funny looks, and harsh comments, and I was so glad I hadn't given up. At the same time, part of me knew this wasn't the end; there was still more I wanted to accomplish as a Bulldog, and I was committed to doing so.

When you finally accomplish a large milestone, enjoy every minute of the experience while also being aware of the whole goal, of everything you dreamed of doing. Don't be satisfied until you achieve all of it.

CHAPTER 8

PEAKS AND VALLEYS

Our greatest glory is not in never falling, but in rising every time we fall.

—CONFUCIUS

Early in the fourth quarter, we trailed twelfth-ranked Arkansas 24-10. Our next drive stalled, and we turned the ball over on downs. Our defense stopped Arkansas and gave the offense a chance to score. We flew down the field in six plays, scored a touchdown, and closed the gap to seven points. On Arkansas's next possession, we stopped them again, got the ball, and marched down the field for another touchdown. Tie score: 24-24.

Our defense was on fire, and they again stopped the Arkansas offense. When we got the ball back this time, however, we couldn't convert and had to punt from midfield. Arkansas took over deep in their own territory with less than a minute on the clock. Now we just had to hold them to force overtime.

Unfortunately, that was the moment our defense collapsed. We gave up three long pass plays in a row, the last one being an easy touchdown to win the game. For the first time since 1993—when I was only four years old—the Georgia Bulldogs started 0–2 in conference play.

Where was I when this frustrating loss happened? Sitting in the stands. Not on the sidelines with my teammates, but in the stands, like any other fan, like my seven-year-old self attending games with my dad. I had put in the work, I had made the team, and I was practicing with my teammates every day, but I still wasn't on the dress list for most games that season. In making the team, I had achieved the major part of my goal and I was thrilled with my accomplishment. But I wasn't satisfied. I wanted to play.

A ROCKY START

The 2010 season did not start as expected. In the preseason we were ranked twenty-first; after easily beating Louisiana-Lafayette, however, we lost the next three games to South Carolina, Arkansas, and Mississippi State. In three short weeks, we had gone from a top-twenty-five team to the team with the worst conference record in the SEC.

With each loss, I felt my chances of playing slipping away. In the very first game against Louisiana-Lafayette, I'd hoped I might get to play because we were up by so many points. But there are guys who have dressed out for years and not played, so I also knew I wasn't high on the priority list in terms of getting in the game.

Then I thought if we had a great season and won a bunch of games, I'd be able to rotate in. But we were falling further away from our team goals every week. I knew that when we did actually get some big wins, the coaches would want to make a statement, and that might not involve rotating in the third- and fourth-string players.

Things did not improve after our loss to Mississippi State. We played Colorado next, a team that was also struggling and fired its coach at the end of the season. We fell behind right away, 14–3, but managed to pull it together after that and scored three touchdowns in a row to go up 24–14. Just when it seemed like we were on a roll, Colorado scored fifteen points in a little over six minutes to retake the lead. We responded with a field goal, so we were down by two points late in the fourth quarter. We got the ball back and drove into field-goal range. With one of the best kickers in the country, it seemed to be a done deal. Then we fumbled the ball and Colorado recovered. When time expired, Colorado fans rushed the field. With that loss, our record dropped to 1–4. In response to the game, future

Pro Bowler A. J. Green said, "I've never been one and four at anything in my life." Georgia hadn't lost four games in a row since the early 1970s.

The beginning of that season was tough. We weren't getting blown out by anyone. We were in each game, but we just kept fumbling the ball or giving up a score at the last second. Our team was at a low point. We were desperate for a win. That desperation showed the next week against Tennessee, when we exploded for a 27–7 lead at halftime. We kept rolling in the second half and ended up winning 41–14 to finally bring the losing streak to an end.

SCOUT TEAM

The Monday following Tennessee, I was told I would be helping out on the offensive line during practice because we had several injured players. Up to that point, I had been running plays on the defensive scout team, simulating what our opponent would do. I hadn't played offensive line since eighth grade, but I was used to studying the position on film from a defensive perspective. I spent the next several weeks flip-flopping between offensive and defensive line, helping out wherever needed.

On the scout team, our job was to study and simulate the opponent we would be facing the following week. We had help from the coaches, who reviewed dozens of hours of film and then created a three-ring binder of plays run by that week's opponent. The graduate assistant coach would hold up a play card and tell us, "Here's what you're running." The whole point was to get the starters as ready as possible for the upcoming game. It was a difficult matchup for third stringers like me. As members of the scout team, we got dominated on most plays.

In practice, I regularly took on double-team blocks from guys like Ben Jones, Cordy Glenn, and Clint Boling, each of whom has started at least six seasons in the NFL as of 2018. They all weighed around 330, compared to my 260. Coaches didn't expect us to win matchups like this, but they did expect top effort.

At this point my speed had increased, but I probably wasn't faster than some of those three-hundred-pound linemen. They could move despite their size. I might beat them in a 110-yard sprint, but on the field we weren't running more than ten yards a play, so sometimes I was still at a disadvantage.

Several times that season, I broke through and beat one-on-one pass protection and tagged off on the quarterback. We didn't tackle the quarterback in practice; we tagged him like you would in a two-hand touch game. Even if I didn't break through, I learned to hold my hands up and try to get in the passing lane. I was able to knock passes to the ground on several occasions.

MIXED EMOTIONS

At this point in the season, the conference championship seemed out of the question. We were 2-4 when we played Vanderbilt, and ended up dominating 43-0. I was thrilled with the score, but I was also thinking, *Man, it would have been nice to dress out for a win like that.* I knew the odds were slim of getting into a game when we were only 2-4, but that's the type of lead where it might happen. I couldn't help feeling disappointed, like my dream was still slightly out of reach even though I had mounted the biggest hurdle of making the team.

After Vanderbilt, we played Kentucky. In scouting, our coaches picked up on the fact that the run would work well against their defense, so we had an extremely run-heavy game plan. Washaun Ealey, one of our running backs, set a single-game school record with five rushing touchdowns. We ended up winning 44-31. We were now 4-4 for the season. At the same time, other teams in our division started losing. We started thinking maybe we could turn this season around and possibly even win the SEC East division title.

Next we faced Florida, our biggest rival. Florida was

having a season similar to ours and had just lost three in a row. Whoever lost this game was out of the division championship race. They jumped out to a 21–7 lead heading into halftime. In the second half, our offense kicked in and scored twenty-four points to force a tie at 31–31 and send the game into overtime. Unfortunately, we didn't score on our possession and Florida did, so we lost 34–31. At that point, the only thing we could play for was enough wins to get into a bowl game.

Every Wednesday before a game, the coaches posted the dress list. And every Wednesday, I went to the locker room to check the list. Some weeks I knew there was zero chance I would be on that list—for example, if we were playing a conference road game and could only take sixty-five guys. When I wasn't on the list for nonconference home games, it was tougher to accept. Nine games into the season, I'd only dressed out for the first game.

The week after Florida, we played Idaho State in a nonconference home game, which meant there was a greater chance I'd be able to dress out. The Wednesday before the game, I went to the locker room as usual to check the dress list. About twenty guys were standing around the page, so I worked my way toward the front. My name was not on the list. I was disappointed, but I knew several walk-ons hadn't dressed out yet this season, so the coaches were trying to give everyone that opportunity.

Walk-ons who started on special teams were always on the dress list. After that, the coaches went by seniority and who added the most value.

We beat Idaho State easily, 55-7, and then turned our sights to our next big game: Auburn. They were ranked number two in the country, had a 10-0 record, and Cam Newton was their quarterback. No one outside the program expected us to win, especially coming in with a 5-5 record.

We jumped out to a 21-7 lead in the second quarter, but Auburn quickly answered and tied it up by halftime. We kept it close for most of the second half, but then our defense became tired and gave up several touchdowns. We ended up losing 49-31, the first time in four years that we had lost to Auburn.

In the last game of the regular season, we played Georgia Tech—a must-win situation if we wanted to go to a bowl game. It was a close back-and-forth game, but we ended up winning by eight and were invited to the Liberty Bowl.

LIBERTY BOWL

After the Georgia Tech game, we had exams and a couple of weeks of practice. Then the coaches posted the Liberty Bowl dress list, and I was on it.

We got to go home a few days before Christmas, and then we were to make our way to Memphis on December 26. Since Memphis is roughly a six-hour drive from Atlanta, I rode with two other walk-ons who lived near me.

The night we arrived, we checked in to the Peabody Hotel and then attended a team welcome dinner and meeting. The next morning, we got up early, ate breakfast as a team, and attended meetings, before being bused over to a local high school for practice. After practice, we ate lunch and then had more meetings—both as a whole team and divided into position groups.

We followed this same schedule all week, and after each day's football work was done, we attended a team event. One night, we saw a Memphis Grizzlies basketball game, and at halftime two guys from our team—A. J. Green and Washaun Ealey—had a shootout against two guys from our bowl opponent, Central Florida. Another night, we met the St. Louis Cardinals minor league baseball team and hit baseballs in their cages. We also attended a rodeo. The whole week was such a fun experience.

Then game day came, December 31, 2010. I had never traveled to an away game or been on the field of a college stadium other than Georgia's, and now I was dressing out for a bowl game. It felt surreal.

That morning, I got up and had breakfast with my team-mates and then went to position meetings. After lunch, we boarded buses at the hotel and headed to Liberty Bowl Memorial Stadium, where our pads and uniforms were waiting in the locker room. This was only the second time I'd seen a Bulldog jersey with my name hanging in the locker. About a half hour before taking the field for warm-ups, I started putting my pads and jersey on. We wore white away jerseys, which was a first for me.

The stadium was just over three-quarters filled. This was before UCF became a household name in football, so more than half of the stadium was filled with Georgia fans, my family among them.

Like any other game day, we went onto the field in position groups for warm-ups and drills. The coach held out a ball and pantomimed snapping it. When he did so, we were supposed to fire off the line for about five yards. We also ran through a couple of light-contact drills. Then the whole team came together to practice running a few plays. Finally, we jogged off the field and gathered in the tunnel to wait for our time to run out together.

We ran out to cheering and noise, but nothing like my first experience running out against Louisiana-Lafayette. There's so much hype around the first game of the season. Plus, this was a bowl game in a smaller stadium against a relatively unknown team, and we had just finished a disappointing 6–6 season. The atmosphere among Georgia fans was warm. It's not that they were fair-weather fans—they'd traveled six hours to Memphis, after all—but when a team has its worst season in more than a decade, people are less likely to go crazy and jump for joy when players run onto the field.

Early in the first quarter, our offense put together a good drive and scored a field goal. Then we just stalled out. Their offense wasn't doing much better, and at halftime it was tied 3–3.

From my place on the sideline, watching the game was a whole different experience than watching it from the stands. The action was right there, and it was loud and intense: the sound of shoulder pads crashing and whistles blowing and guys breathing heavy as they sprinted off the field.

Every time the defense came off the field, the defensive line gathered around Coach Garner. He took out a whiteboard and asked the players what they were seeing and drew up plans for what to do next time. From where I stood off to the side, I caught a word here and there. I wanted so badly to be in that group. I wanted to be the one sharing what I saw and receiving direction to put into action when I went back onto the field. I knew that next year was my final season to make that happen.

After halftime, we came out and drove down the field on our first possession, but we had to settle for a field goal. Our defense held UCF until the fourth quarter, when they scored the only touchdown of the game. We lost 10-6. That was UCF's first bowl win in school history, and it was not the kind of performance our team expected to have. It was a quiet locker room and a long ride back to the hotel.

That loss capped a season of peaks and valleys. I had made the team and experienced so many incredible high points: first fall practice season, first game dressing out, and first bowl game. I was thrilled to be part of this group of guys who felt like family. But there were a lot of disappointments, too. On a personal level, I would have liked to dress out more. While practices were fun, they were nothing compared to the excitement of a game. As a team, we hit some historic low points:

- Before this season, Georgia had only lost to Arkansas three times in school history.
- Mississippi State had not beaten Georgia in Starkville since 1951; my parents weren't even born then.
- This was the first season since I was seven years old that Georgia didn't win at least eight games.
- We made it to a bowl game and then lost to a team that had never won a bowl game in school history.
- Since I was a freshman, Georgia's win total had

dropped each year: first it was eleven, then ten, then eight, and finally six.

I was thankful my journey didn't end there. My goal wasn't truly complete. It wouldn't be until I ran onto the field and played in a game.

YOUR TURN

Even though I achieved my goal of being a Georgia Bulldog, it wasn't all sunshine and rainbows. I didn't get to play in my first season, and the team didn't win as much as we'd hoped. Life is like that. There are peaks and valleys, and sometimes they are right next to each other. You have to take the bad with the good and keep pressing forward.

People don't hit their personal best every time. Think of a runner who wins his first race. He's not guaranteed to win every race after that. Some days, he's going to come up short. Winning the first race for me was making the team; that was the biggest part of my goal. But I still had a lot of work to do if I was going to realize my dream in full and actually get into a game.

Just as it's easy to let success inflate your ego, it's easy to let failure lead to discouragement and giving up. However, if you approach both success and failure as motivation to stay determined and hardworking, you will remain steady in your thoughts and focused on the end goal.

CHAPTER 9

1,543 DAYS

What you get by achieving your goals is not as important as what you become by achieving your goals.

—HENRY DAVID THOREAU

Within a week of the bowl game, we were back at school, ready to start a new football season. We all took a seat and chatted while we waited for the meeting to begin. When Coach Richt walked in, the room fell silent.

"Hello, everyone," Coach said as he looked around the room. "Good to see you all. I hope you enjoyed the last few days with family. I want to welcome the freshmen in the room who have joined us early, and we will have more recruits joining us this fall. It's time to turn the page and put together a good season, starting right here and now."

Coach didn't dwell on last season. He didn't mention

how poorly we'd done or even what lessons we could pull from that experience. He dove right into what we were going to accomplish this year, and the whole room was right with him. He talked about the new facilities, the new weight room, and the new incoming recruiting class, already dubbed the Dream Team. His words set the tone of looking forward to a promising new season.

When Coach finished, we went to our position-group meetings, which were held in the newly renovated football facility. None of us had been in there yet. We looked around, amazed. Instead of dark gray walls, there were murals of past legends in Georgia history. It gave you a sense that since these guys were sitting in the same building and are now playing in the NFL, you could do that, too. We also toured the rest of the new football facility, including the state-of-the-art weight room.

Everything about that first day back had a new feel to it, from the facilities, to the players, to the attitudes. On a personal level, this was my first time showing up in January as part of the team, not someone trying out. This was my team and my facility. Now I just had to find a way to play.

SPRING

That spring, I didn't have the pressure of trying out for the team, but I did feel the need to keep improving. I bench-pressed 225 eighteen times, by far the highest number of reps I'd done at that weight. The first year I tried out, I could barely lift 225 once.

From the start of spring workouts, there was a lot of emphasis on our first two games of the season. Boise State was going to be highly ranked in the preseason, and they were our first opponent of 2011. TVs in the new facility displayed an ongoing countdown to the game: 190 days, five hours, six minutes, thirty-two seconds until kickoff. In addition, Boise State highlight reels ran on the TVs in the weight room. Months before the actual game, we were well aware of how significant that opening matchup was.

South Carolina was our second game; they had just won the SEC East for the first time in school history, and they were returning many key players. We didn't have a tune-up game to start the season like last year with Louisiana-Lafayette. We played some amazing teams right off the bat.

During my first two years of spring workouts, we had a decent weight room. While the new one was under construction during the 2010 season, we used an old weight room under the bleachers in the basketball coliseum. Now, we were in a brand-new facility that was brighter, more spacious, and packed with equipment. It radiated hope, new beginnings, and new possibilities.

In general, I saw more action in spring practices and drills. The first two years I had tried out, I was considered fourth or fifth string. Coaches don't give regular reps to people below third string. As fourth or fifth string, I would rotate in every third time when they called for the threes. Now I was officially third string and took all of the reps with the threes.

I also saw more action in the spring game that year. I took it as a sign that the coaches trusted me to execute the plays, at least in a spring-game setting.

Spring game my senior year, April 2011.

SUMMER

After finals ended, we were allowed to go home for the rest of May. I went back to Atlanta and worked out with

Jarrett again. I returned to campus in June and trained with the team through the end of July.

During the season, it's hard to keep on weight, let alone bulk up, because you're practicing four hours a day, sweating and burning off calories. Because of this, the offseason is the time to gain weight. At the end of my summer workouts, I had reached 265 pounds, my heaviest to date.

I was still eating ten meals a day. I had continued that all the way through last season because it was the only way to keep weight on. I probably would have dropped fifteen pounds a week for the first couple of weeks if I hadn't kept eating that much. The number of calories I had to consume just to stay above 250 was ridiculous.

FOOTBALL CAMP

At the end of July, coaches posted the list of players going to camp. The team only brings 105 guys to camp in August, and every new preferred walk-on gets to go, so that leaves a few spots for the rest of us. I was really excited to see my name on the list this time.

Camp was exhausting. It was nearly two weeks of nonstop football. We woke up around 6:30 each day and checked in for team breakfast by 7:00. At 8:00 we put on pads, at 8:30 we had meetings, and by 10:00 we were on the practice field. Around 1:30 we stopped for lunch, and then we had time for a nap. My dorm was a twenty-minute walk away, so I just stayed at the football facility and napped on a couch. Later in the afternoon, we had team meetings, dinner, position meetings, and nightly walk-throughs, where we ran through plays at half speed with no tackling. Walk-throughs didn't end until midnight, and then we had to wake up the next day at 6:30 and repeat the grueling program.

It was ridiculously hot that August—more than 100 degrees the first few days, but it felt like 120 on the Astro-Turf surrounded by concrete walls. The first day involved a conditioning test: groups of players ran 220-yard sprints for time. If anyone in the group failed to finish under the designated time, the whole group repeated the drill. It was similar to the conditioning test at the end of summer workouts last year. We were only wearing helmets, shorts, and jerseys for practice that day—no pads—and we still had three defensive linemen fall out due to heat exhaustion. I ended up taking reps with the second string for the first few days because the team was missing so many defensive linemen.

When I was on scout team, I knew I needed to give my best, but I wasn't that heavily scrutinized. When I started taking reps with the second string in practice, however,

I felt a lot more pressure. Second stringers were held to a higher standard; they were expected to hold their own against the starters.

After every practice during camp, Coach Richt had a list of people the media wanted to interview. At the end of the second day, he called my name. My head snapped up. *They want to talk to me?* The guys next to me turned to stare; they seemed just as surprised as I was.

I had no idea what to do, so I asked one of the starters, "Hey, where do I go? I've never been interviewed before."

"Go up to the second floor, near the trophy room," he replied.

I thanked him and headed upstairs. There I found out that I was being interviewed by the school newspaper, the *Red & Black*, for an article on Georgia football walk-ons. I was excited they were doing this. Since college football teams have eighty-five scholarship players, walk-ons generally don't see much playing time. Other sports like golf or tennis might only have a handful of scholarships to hand out, so walk-ons might still be some of the best players on the team.

The interviewer asked me questions such as "What was your experience like, being a walk-on?" and "What are some of the things that motivate you?" The paper ran the article the next day and included my answer to the question "What was it like to dress out for a game?"

> All I wanted to do as a kid was to come to Georgia and play football. I've been dreaming about that every night. Running out on the field, hearing the crowd scream and getting focused and ready to bring home a win for Georgia; that was just such an amazing experience. Words can't even describe how great it was. I watched so many guys on TV wear that same uniform I got to wear. So I really felt blessed to have the chance to do that.

Over the course of camp, we had several scrimmages in the stadium, and I got in for a few plays, and even beat a block and tackled the running back for a five-yard loss on one play. My position coach, the athletic trainer, and a few teammates noticed and congratulated me. To break through like that on one of only a few plays felt great.

On the last few nights of camp, we did something called the hot seat. Leaders on the team, usually juniors or seniors, went in front of the group, sat in the "hot seat," and talked about what Georgia meant to them, what motivated them, and so on. Three guys spoke each night. Some guys shared meaningful thoughts on their road to Georgia; others talked about the upcoming season.

I really wanted to get up there and say something, but I knew it was usually the captains and starters who shared. On the last night, there was a decent pause, so I decided to go for it. I stood up and walked toward the front. A couple of people started clapping; they wanted to hear what I had to say.

I took a seat and shared my story, starting from when I was a kid going to football games with my dad. I talked about high school and college and how I only ever wanted to go to Georgia.

"Most of you guys could have played anywhere—LSU, Alabama, Ohio State, Texas. You all probably had really long highlight tapes. I didn't have any because I was fourth-string my senior year of high school and only got to play when we were up by thirty points or more. I recorded zero tackles as a senior. No college wanted me to play on their team. I knew I wanted to play for Georgia, and it was a matter of me working hard and never giving up. This is why you guys see me in the dining hall eating all the time. I gained 120 pounds over the last four years.

"When I wasn't in class, I was literally spending every second of my day working out, eating, running—doing something related to making this team. It was tough trying out and getting cut, then trying out a second time and getting cut again. But I refused to back down. I found a way to come back bigger, faster, and stronger, and I finally made it."

All eyes were on me. Although I knew every player on the team, most of them didn't know my whole story. I could tell they were really paying attention.

"Georgia football means so much to me. Despite everything I've done, my main contribution to this team is getting you guys ready to play. If it means that much to me, to just be able to get other people ready to play, think about what it means to you guys, to be the ones out there starting for this team. I dedicated three years of my life to figuring out what in the world I could do to make this team, to be able to play alongside this group of guys, and be coached by these coaches. I am so thankful for this opportunity."

When I finished, everyone clapped, just as they did for each person who spoke. Cornelius Washington, one of the starting outside linebackers, approached me in the hallway afterward and said he had no idea I had gone through all of that.

Three years later, I worked with a guy who was a graduate assistant coach when I played for Georgia. He told me that my hot seat speech was one of the best speeches he'd ever seen anyone give. It really touched me that three years later he still remembered it.

That night, we did one more team-bonding activity: we watched *Courageous*, a movie directed by, written by, and starring Alex Kendrick. I remembered him from watching *Facing the Giants*, another inspirational movie. Alex actually came to the viewing with his son. It was a great way to end camp.

MY FINAL SEASON

Over the summer, Coach Richt had the whole team read a book called *The Energy Bus*. The book discussed the importance of fueling your life and your team with positive energy and calling out "energy vampires"—those who suck energy out of the team. That fall, if someone was late for a meeting or said something negative, his picture appeared on the locker-room TV screens with the words "energy vampire" underneath. It was a fun reminder of the new positive energy we wanted to have this season.

Defensive line on picture day, August 2011. Back row, left to right: graduate assistant coach Brandon Wheeling, Derrick Lott, Geoff Rapp, Kwame Geathers, Garrison Smith, and defensive line coach Rodney Garner. Front row, left to right: John Jenkins, Mike Thornton, me, DeAngelo Tyson, and Abry Jones.

Picture day, August 2011. I'm standing with my sisters (from the left) Courtlyn, Carsen, and Cayden.

One morning during preseason practice, we received a text from one of the coaches:

> Do you love football? Because today we GET to play some football. Today we GET to be Bulldogs. Don't take it for granted.

I loved the message. It perfectly expressed what I was already thinking: I had exactly three and a half months left until I was no longer a Georgia football player. This was it. This was my last chance to make everything happen football-wise. I needed to take advantage of it.

One morning at the dining hall that fall, Rex Bradberry, an assistant strength coach, walked in. He was checking on players as they ate breakfast to make sure nobody skipped a meal. If you're attempting workouts as grueling as ours, skipping meals is the last thing you should be doing.

As I sat down with several teammates, Coach Bradberry looked at me and announced to the table, "This is the most dedicated guy on the team right here." A couple of the guys looked up and nodded. It felt good to have my hard work acknowledged. I clearly wasn't the best player, but the guys knew I put more effort into preparing than anyone else did.

Fan day with my good friend John Huff, August 2011. John later tried out for and made the Georgia football team for the 2014 and 2015 seasons.

Signing autographs on fan day, August 2011.

BOISE STATE

The Boise State game had been hyped since spring, and to add to the excitement, we were playing the game in Atlanta at the old Georgia Dome. In addition, Nike decided to release new uniforms for both schools. We would be wearing red pants, which Georgia hadn't worn since the 1970s, and red jerseys that all said "Georgia" across the back instead of our last names. We had gray helmets with a red stripe down the middle. Some people described them as storm-trooper helmets. We also had new gloves that formed the Georgia G when you put your hands together. And the topper, as far as I was concerned: I was dressing out for the game. I couldn't have been more excited. I grew up in Atlanta; my parents and sisters still lived there. It was a nonconference game, but we still didn't take much more than eighty-five guys, and I was one of them.

At the team lunch before the Boise State game, we were talking about practice the previous day. All of a sudden Wes Van Dyk, one of my teammates, told me in front of the whole group, "You've gotten a lot better as a football player." That's not something the guys usually said to each other, and it meant a lot that other people recognized the progress I had made.

Boise State was ranked fifth in the country to start the season; we were ranked nineteenth. For me to be able to dress out for that game in my hometown against a top-five team was amazing. Beyond just this game, it was a preview of what was to come: instead of just dressing out for the bare minimum like last year, I might actually be in the rotation to dress out more often.

Even though Atlanta was a neutral site for the game, the crowd was 80 percent Georgia fans because Atlanta is so close to the university. The Dome was smaller than our home field, but it was still incredibly loud because it was enclosed.

Either because of the noise or because of big-game jitters, our offense false-started a few times at the beginning of the game and had a hard time getting things moving on the first two drives. The coaches decided to try something completely different and used a defensive player, Brandon Boykin, on offense. The quarterback handed Boykin the ball, and he was off for an eighty-yard run to the end zone. With that one run, Boykin ended up being our leading rusher for the entire game. Boise State responded with a touchdown and then got another one right before halftime to go up 14-7.

In the second half, Boise State started to pull away and led 35-14 going into the fourth quarter. We scored one more touchdown to make it 35-21, but that was all our offense could muster.

Being on the sidelines in my hometown was amazing—the electric atmosphere in the Georgia Dome, the new uniforms, and the excitement of the new season. But it stunk to lose. Following the game, the team was disappointed, naturally, but no one was about to throw in the towel on the season.

SOUTH CAROLINA

Our first SEC game was against South Carolina, who was ranked twelfth in the country. The Wednesday before the game, I checked the dress list: my name was not there.

The next day I got a call from the director of football operations. I had no idea why he was calling me.

"Hi, Candler," he said. "Listen. One of the players has decided not to dress out tomorrow. You're the next person in line."

I was dumbfounded. I could not imagine why someone would choose not to dress out. Even if you're hurt, you would still want to be out there in your jersey and shorts.

"Great," I replied. "Thank you."

I immediately called my parents. "Hey. I hope you're still free on Saturday. I'm dressing out for the game!"

Along with Boise State, South Carolina was one of the most anticipated games of the season. One of my best friends, Ryan Manthey, went to the University of South Carolina and was from Atlanta. He showed up at Dawg Walk dressed in South Carolina gear and carrying a sign that read "Candler Cook for Heisman," waving it proudly as I walked off the bus with my teammates.

Before the Georgia–South Carolina game, September 10, 2011.

The game started with some solid drives, but we just couldn't finish them and had to settle for field goals. After the second one, we tried an onside kick and recovered it—only to have it called back for an offsides penalty. After the penalty, South Carolina marched the ball down the field for a touchdown. We answered right back, and then they did the same, so we were losing 14–13 at halftime.

In the second half, we continued going back and forth, and near the beginning of the fourth quarter we tied it at 28–28 with a two-point conversion. Then they hit a long field goal and we answered with a touchdown, so we were up 35–31 with six minutes left in the game. And then we were visited by the ghost of last year's games. South Carolina scored a touchdown, and when it was our turn, the quarterback got sacked and fumbled the ball.

South Carolina recovered and immediately returned it for a touchdown. We scored one more time, but it wasn't enough, and we lost 45–42.

To be so close and have it slip away yet again was devastating. At this point, talk on campus started turning negative. People were saying things like "Here we go again" and "The coaches need to be fired." As a team, we were disappointed, but not negative. We were still hanging on to the new vibe, the energy bus.

And soon everything turned around.

WINNING STREAK

In the next game, we beat Coastal Carolina 59–0. I dressed out for the game and really hoped to get in because we were up by so much, but it didn't happen. It was our first big lead of the season, and we had a lot of young scholarship players who were getting their first game reps. Then we beat Ole Miss on the road 27–13.

The next week, I dressed out for the Mississippi State home game. Before the team ran onto the field, I positioned myself at the corner of the locker room closest to the field, so I was one of the first players to run through the banner. It was incredible. When you start running, you can't see anything, and then all of a sudden you burst through and the fans, mascot, and cheerleaders come into focus. It was an amazing experience.

During warm-ups, Mississippi State was huddled together near midfield, jumping up and down and getting themselves pumped. The problem from our perspective was that they were stomping on the Georgia G.

We were supposed to be focused on warm-ups, but our guys were getting angry. Finally, our defensive coordinator stopped warm-ups as a player yelled, "Push them off the G!" and our whole team rushed over to meet them at midfield.

It was like a scene out of the movie *300*, where the Spartans are pushing the Persians off the cliff. We formed a wall and started shoving the Mississippi State players off of the G. It was pretty intense.

The same day that we beat Mississippi State, South Carolina lost to Auburn and Florida lost to Alabama, putting us into a three-way tie for first in the SEC East.

The week before we played Tennessee, Coach Richt stopped me as I was walking out of the building after practice and said, "Candler, I want you to know that I really appreciate what you're doing for this team." That meant so much coming from him. The fact that he took notice of every player on the team like that says a lot about him. That Saturday we beat Tennessee to give Coach Richt his one hundredth win as Georgia's head coach.

The following week we played Vanderbilt, which should have been a comfortable win, but late in the fourth quarter, we let a sixteen-point lead to shrink to five. With less than a minute left, Vanderbilt blocked our punt. All of a sudden it seemed like last year all over again, when we couldn't close out a game. Our punter managed to grab the shoe of the Vanderbilt player who had recovered the ball, preventing him from running all the way for a touchdown. Vanderbilt tried multiple passes to the end zone in the waning seconds, but we ended up hanging on for the win.

Florida was next. I traveled to the game in Jacksonville since it was only a five-hour drive from Athens. When I was there, I ran into Drew Williams, a former Georgia player who had graduated. I confided in him that I was really hoping to play in our next game against New Mexico State. Based on our schedule, I knew that game would be my last chance to step onto the field and play as a Georgia Bulldog. Drew told me, "Make sure your coach knows how badly you want to play. The worst that can happen is you won't get to play anyway. Just be bold about it." I took his advice to heart.

The Florida game didn't start well. We fell behind 17–3 in

the second quarter before facing a crucial fourth down. Since we had already missed a field goal, we decided to go for it this time. Aaron Murray, our quarterback, floated a pass to the corner of the end zone. The ball hung in the air for what seemed like an eternity. Finally, the receiver came down with it for a touchdown. After our defense forced a second fumble, our offense moved the ball and then faced another key fourth down. We elected to go for it again and threw a touchdown pass to tie the game. Late in the fourth quarter, we rode the strength of our running game and went on to win 24–20, with the defense giving up only thirty-two yards in the second half.

Before that game, Florida had won eighteen of the previous twenty-one games in the Georgia–Florida rivalry. For us to come from behind and win was a huge mental victory for the team. Our confidence grew as our record improved to 6–2, and we moved into a two-way tie for first with South Carolina.

NEW MEXICO STATE

The Thursday before the New Mexico State game, I walked into the defensive line meeting room and saw Coach Garner.

"Hey, Coach," I said. "If you get the chance on Saturday, I really want to play in this game."

"Okay, Candler," he said. "There haven't been a lot of big leads this season."

"I know. But in this game, if we get a big lead, I really want to play."

"Okay." I turned to walk out, knowing Coach could tell how important it was to me to play in a game.

That Saturday, I woke up knowing that this was it: I was either going to play today, or I would never play as a Georgia Bulldog. The tough part was knowing there was nothing more I could do to make my goal happen. I had done the work, dedicated the hours, practiced with maximum effort every time, but now the decision was out of my hands. If the starters didn't get a big lead, it didn't matter how badly I wanted to play. It just wouldn't happen.

I went to the dining hall by myself, ate two cups of oatmeal and four egg whites, and drank a quart of whole milk. It was the same breakfast I'd eaten many times over the last few years, but that day felt different. I knew what was about to happen. I told myself to stay positive. Coach Garner knew what I wanted. I knew what I wanted.

After breakfast, I walked over to the football facility listening to "Warrior" by Disturbed. I went through my usual ritual of sitting in the locker room listening to music for a while, and then put on my pads and uniform. Coach Richt addressed the team, reminding us that we needed to win this game to stay on track toward our goals.

We went through the Dawg Walk and then headed into the stadium. We all did some stretching on our own and walked around; I said hi to my parents and sisters as I watched the fans pouring in.

When we ran out of the tunnel, I made sure I was at the front, leading our team onto the field and through the banner. This was it.

We were highly favored over New Mexico State, but we got off to a slow start. This was not good news for me. I needed a blowout to have any chance of getting on that field, and it needed to happen quickly. For a walk-on like me to play, the team needs to have a comfortable lead for a good chunk of the game. Once they do, coaches start putting in some of the freshmen and sophomore scholarship players who don't get a lot of playing time. After that, coaches put in some walk-ons. The key is that the starters needed to pull away with a lot of time left in the game. Early in the second quarter, however, we were only up 7–3, and I was getting nervous.

Suddenly, the offense caught on fire. They scored forty-two unanswered points to pull ahead 49–3. As of 2018, forty-two points is the most ever scored by a Georgia team in a single quarter.

In the third quarter, coaches started rotating in freshmen scholarship guys. We scored another touchdown, so the score was 56–3.

With seven minutes left in the game, Brandon Wheeling, one of the graduate assistants, walked over and said, "Candler, start stretching. You're going in."

If someone had talked to me right after that, I wouldn't have heard a word they said. For the next thirty seconds my head was buzzing. My skin felt hot as I started stretching—after standing on the sideline for three hours, I needed to loosen up again.

It was such a blowout that many fans had left, so my family had moved down to the front row of the fifty-yard line. I turned and waved; they knew that meant I was going in. My friends John and Tyler Huff were also there in the front row cheering for me.

With 5:51 on the clock and the score 63–10, Coach Garner sent me into the game. I sprinted from the sideline to the far hash of the field and into the huddle, my stomach churning. I had to ignore the nerves and think back to every practice, every film session, and every time I had looked through the playbook. I knew the plays; I just needed to focus. The moment was huge, and I knew it would be for the rest of my life, but at that instant I just needed to keep my head in the game and do my job.

Getting to play against New Mexico State, November 5, 2011.

When I got to the huddle, our nose guard said he wanted to line up at defensive end. I knew better than to argue in the huddle, so I lined up at nose guard, which is usually the biggest person on defense—not a 265 pounder like me. I knew if anyone lined up incorrectly, it would be on me since I was the new player being sent in for that drive.

As nose guard, the play called for me to line up opposite the center's outside shoulder, and go to the strong-side B gap between the guard and tackle. As soon as the ball was snapped, I crossed the guard's face and got to the gap. The offense ran a sweep to the strong side, but way outside the gap I was covering. The cornerback made the tackle.

On the next play, our nose guard lined up where he should be, and I lined up at defensive end in a five technique, which is on the outside shoulder of the tackle. My assignment once again was the strong-side B gap. After the ball was hiked, I cut inside to cover my gap. This time New Mexico State ran a handoff to the weak side, so I ran in pursuit, but the ballcarrier was tackled before I got there.

I was subbed out on the next play to let more guys see some action. My adrenaline was still pumping. I had just played in a Georgia football game. The pride I felt wasn't just related to that single moment. It came from every moment when I had the chance to give up or was told to give up and didn't. I kept pushing and pushing, and now I had completely succeeded.

After the game, I showered and turned on my phone. I received a text from Molloy VanGorder, whose dad used to be the defensive coordinator at Georgia. Molloy had been a walk-on a few years earlier when I was trying out. The text said, "Of all the walk-ons, you're my favorite to watch, because I know what you went through." He knew I had worked hard and waited a long time for this moment. It had been 1,543 days since I first walked into Coach T's office to ask about trying out, and now I had officially played in a game. I did it.

YOUR TURN

Achieving your end goal is an amazing feeling. You've been working hard every day, and then you're suddenly there. You overcame the doubt—yours and others'—and went above and beyond to get what you wanted. This is the pinnacle. You made it to the top of the mountain.

Soak it in. Enjoy it. Live in that moment. It will mean more to you than to anyone else because you are the only one who knows every bit of hard work that went into it.

CHAPTER 10

NO REGRETS

The game of life is a lot like football. You have to tackle your problems, block your fears, and score your points when you get the opportunity.

—LEWIS GRIZZARD

The New Mexico State game was the highlight for me, but the 2011 season wasn't over. I was part of a team, and the team victories were an integral part of my personal victories.

The same day we beat New Mexico State, South Carolina lost, giving us sole possession of first place in the SEC East. We had two conference games left—Auburn and Kentucky—and we had to win both to clinch the division title. Auburn had already beat South Carolina, who had beat us at the beginning of the season, so our already heated rivalry with Auburn, the defending national champions, took on even greater significance.

I was awarded scout team player of the week for my contributions in practice to prepare the team to face Auburn, which meant I was guaranteed to dress out that week. That was the first weekly award I had received as a Bulldog.

We jumped out to an early lead, thanks to our offense converting third downs and our defense forcing turnovers. When we went up 21–7, the team was issued a sideline warning because some players were celebrating so close to the field. While the ref was talking to Coach Richt, our defense intercepted the ball and ran it back for a touchdown. At that point, the whole team rushed the field to celebrate. Coach looked at the ref and shrugged, as if to say, "What can you do?" We kept rolling from there and ended up winning 45–7. We were one win away from the SEC East title.

The final SEC game of the regular season was senior day. About fifteen minutes before kickoff, I lined up with the other seniors on the sideline. One by one, I watched my teammates run out onto the field to greet their families, and then it was my turn. Over the loudspeaker I heard, "Candler Cook, defensive end, from Atlanta, Georgia." I ran toward midfield to meet my parents and sisters, and then we took pictures with Coach Richt.

Senior day against Kentucky, November 19, 2011. Standing next to me is my mom, Penni.

After this, we all gathered in the locker room to get ready for kickoff. About five minutes before everyone else ran out onto the field, Coach Richt said, "Okay seniors, head outside."

We jogged over to the sideline and waited for the ref's signal. Then all twenty seniors—scholarship players and walk-ons alike—walked arm in arm to midfield for the coin toss. The fact that I was a captain on my last day playing in Sanford Stadium was really cool.

Kentucky wasn't having a particularly good season, but they were really motivated that day and took an early 10-6 lead. Our defense and special teams forced two turnovers that led to field goals, so we finally pulled ahead

12–10 at halftime. Coach Grantham, the defensive coordinator, pulled the defense aside and emphatically said, "If we don't give up another point, we're going to the SEC championship." Our defense responded and didn't give up another point the rest of the game, and we won 19–10.

As soon as the game ended, the display board showed the Georgia G and the words "SEC East Champions" underneath. The whole team ran over to the student section, where they were going wild. The Georgia fight song blared over the loudspeakers, students high-fived us, and we all soaked up the joy of winning a division title. So many people had doubted us at the beginning of the season after we lost the first two big games, but we proved them wrong.

We took the celebration into the locker room. Coach Richt held up the division championship plaque as the team held him on their shoulders, yelling and cheering. Someone sprayed water on the locker-room floor, and after the team lowered Coach Richt, he ran and belly-slid across the room. The team went nuts.

Our final regular season game was against Georgia Tech. I didn't dress out, because it was on the road. With that win, we had won ten games in a row. As of 2018, that's still the most consecutive wins in one season for a Georgia football team since 1982.

THE SEC CHAMPIONSHIP GAME

I really wanted to dress out for the SEC championship, but I knew they could only dress out eighty-five guys. I had never been on the travel list for a road game. I had only gone to the Liberty Bowl the year before because the team could dress an unlimited number of players.

The Wednesday before the game, I walked into the locker room to check the list, because that's what I did before every game, no matter how slim my chances were of being on it. My name was there. I couldn't believe it. I was part of the eighty-five. I was taking a scholarship player's place.

Friday night, the team was bused to Atlanta. The game was at the Georgia Dome, where we had played Boise State in the first game of the season. Our opponent: LSU. No one outside the program gave us a chance. LSU was undefeated and ranked number one in the country.

An hour or so before the game, we got to walk around the field. I reflected on how awesome it was to be here. Some walk-ons don't want to be redshirted; they would rather forfeit a year of eligibility. Had I done that, I wouldn't have played in a college football game. I wouldn't have been in the Dome that night, one of eighty-five guys dressing out for Georgia in the SEC championship game.

The Georgia Dome was filled to capacity, and at least half were Georgia fans. We started strong and went up by a field goal. Then we executed a trick onside kick that left LSU stunned. We recovered the ball and marched down the field but ended up missing a field goal attempt. Later we added a touchdown to go up 10-0. Though we missed opportunities to put more points on the board, LSU's offense couldn't get anything going. They didn't record a first down until the third quarter.

In the second half, however, our offense shut down and didn't score any more. LSU scored twenty-one points off of turnovers, and an additional fourteen were scored on or set up by punt returns. Our defense played very well, giving up only fifty-three passing yards and one third down conversion in the entire game, but they couldn't make up the difference. We ended up getting blown out 42-10, even though we outgained them on offense.

It was tough to watch us lose when it seemed like we had a great game plan, but I was so thankful to be part of the experience. I was part of this team, in wins and in losses. Whatever was happening, I was a full-fledged part of the group that was accomplishing it.

I was no longer an outsider. I was a Georgia Bulldog.

Bobby Short, one of my fraternity brothers, sat in the very

front row at the game, shouting and pointing at me. After the game, he sent me a message:

> Speaking on behalf of the rest of the brotherhood, we are really proud of you. I just want to tell you that before you graduate. I've never met anyone in my entire life who has worked as hard as you have to reach your goal, and seeing you on the sideline at the SEC championship definitely made me proud to tell my dad that one of my brothers is out there living his dream.

THE AWARDS BANQUET

The week after the SEC championship game, we had the awards banquet. The seniors all received a plaque and a framed red jersey showing our name and number. I also received an award: the Iron Man trophy. It's awarded to players who go through the whole season without being late or missing a single event: practice, workout, camp, class, and anything else football related. Even if you have extenuating circumstances—if you're sick or have to go to a wedding—you aren't eligible. Twelve guys received it that season. I wasn't eligible the year before because I wasn't one of the 105 invited to camp.

Awards banquet, December 2011. My dad, Gregg, is holding my letterman's plaque. I'm holding my Iron Man trophy.

At the banquet, they showed a highlight video of each senior consisting of pictures from the time they were a baby to present day. The moms provided the pictures and put the video together. It was cool to see the transformations that some other players made from middle school and high school to college.

THE OUTBACK BOWL

The last game of my senior season was the Outback Bowl in Tampa, Florida. As with the Liberty Bowl, we had events planned alongside the practices and meetings. We attended two dinners sponsored by Outback Steakhouse, and we went to a Tampa Bay Lightning hockey game, the beach, and Busch Gardens. It was a fun week.

We practiced at the University of Tampa. During my last practice as a Georgia Bulldog, we did a one-on-one pass rush drill. I ended up winning both of my reps, a great way to finish off my final drill.

We played the game on the Tampa Bay Buccaneers' home field, which has a unique layout with a pirate ship in one end zone. The game went back and forth, and we ended up surrendering a sixteen-point lead and losing to Michigan State 33-30 in triple overtime. We finished the season 10-4.

As I walked off the field that day, I was happy. Normally I'm pretty downtrodden after a loss, but not that day. It was my last time walking off the field as a Bulldog, and I had done everything I set out to do. That season I dressed out for nine games and, most importantly, played in one. There wasn't anything I could have done to make myself any better or to make the experience any sweeter. I put it all out there, and it had paid off.

After the bowl game, I met with the other seniors to design the SEC championship rings, which we received the following March. That ring represents years of hard work—years I put in to help myself and this program as much as possible. It represents the fact that I never gave up or let anyone stand in the way of my goal. I would not be denied.

Standing with head coach Mark Richt at my college graduation, December 2011.

YOUR TURN

As your journey comes to an end, take time to reflect: What lessons did you learn? What would you do differently next time? How will this experience influence your life going forward?

I have absolutely no regrets about the hours, days, and years I invested in making my dream a reality. Beyond the immediate satisfaction of being on the team and playing in a game, achieving my goal has influenced my life today for the better. I learned to think outside the box and see things through to the end, both of which I now use at work and in other everyday situations. I also learned to embrace hard work, both inside and outside the weight room. I have continued working out and eating healthy, but now I do it to stay in shape and not to increase numbers.

Once you identify the lessons you've learned, find ways to apply them to other areas of your life and in your pursuit of future goals. You will always face obstacles, and having a toolkit of ways to confront them will come in handy.

CONCLUSION

Each of us has a spark of life inside us, and our highest endeavor ought to be to set off that spark in one another.

—KENNY AUSUBEL

As a member of the football team, I attended Faculty Appreciation Day practices for faculty and their families. One professor brought his son John to several events, and we became friends. John was four years younger than I was and shared my lifelong passion for Georgia football.

A couple of years after I graduated, John transferred to Georgia with one goal in mind: to become a walk-on football player. He looked to me for advice, and I provided him information I had learned throughout my journey: when the tryout meeting was, what workouts were like, what happened at mat drills, and what to expect at spring practice. John made the team and enjoyed the same experience I did, helping on scout team at practice and dressing out for several games.

To be able to share what I'd learned and help John chase down his dream was incredibly rewarding. And that's what I hope this book does for you.

What goal have you been putting off because it seems too ridiculous or difficult? Flip the switch in your mind; instead of focusing on why it's impossible, start thinking of ways to make it happen. You don't want to get to the end of your life and think about what could have been. As a wise person once said, "One day your life will flash before your eyes. Make sure it's worth watching."

Start by finding out what you want—not what you might like to buy this week, but what you truly want out of life. Nobody else can help you find that; it must come from within. If you have a hard time pinpointing it, then take a minute to clear your mind. Sit down, close your eyes, put your phone on silent, and think about what makes you feel happy and alive. Imagine yourself doing that at the highest level. Imagine that being your reality every day. Those images will show you what you truly want.

Next, make a plan. What will it take to get you from where you are now to where you want to be? Do research, find out the requirements, and put together a strategy for making it happen. Make that plan a priority, and don't let unimportant things get in your way.

As you progress, don't allow yourself to get complacent. Enjoy the successes, but keep your goal in the forefront of your mind and strive to get closer every day. When your dream finally becomes a reality, soak it in. You alone will know the sacrifices that went into getting there.

I have always believed that superhuman levels of hard work and discipline will triumph over a high level of talent that isn't putting in the same level of effort. So many players were better than me at football, but they didn't eat right, they skipped reps in the weight room when the coach wasn't looking, or they didn't run on their own time. As a result, they left a huge gap for someone like me who was working hard to make the team, potentially in their place. I am living proof that consistently doing the little things right matters and that no obstacle is too big to overcome.

Sanford Stadium, November 2012. The mural shows me, number 98, leading the team onto the field during our fall 2011 game against Auburn. The mural stayed up through the 2016 season.

ACKNOWLEDGMENTS

Trying out for the team the first time was both nerve-wracking and exciting, and going through it with my good friend Brian Pelon kept me motivated even during moments of doubt. Brian, you were the first friend I made at Georgia, and you stood by me through all of the struggles and successes. Thank you.

Craig Sager Jr., you handed me the keys to improving myself through training and nutrition. There is no way I would have made the team without the knowledge you gave me and the hours we spent training together.

Jarrett Moore, thank you for helping me push through plateaus and find a new gear within myself. Your encouragement and positive attitude are contagious.

John Huff, you're the reason I wrote this book. Serving as

your mentor during the tryout and walk-on process and seeing you fulfill your dream inspired me to publish my journey as a roadmap to help others achieve their dreams as well. You're as loyal and hardworking as anyone I've ever met, and it brought me great joy to play even a small part in your success.

A special thanks to my position coach, Rodney Garner, who took a chance on an undersized, unathletic defensive end and helped me fulfill my dream. I am eternally grateful to you for putting me into the New Mexico State game my senior year. Your coaching taught me lessons that have continued to last long after I finished playing football.

Coach Todd Grantham, thank you for letting me be part of your defense. In your very first practice at Georgia, I messed up in a drill and you got onto me about it. A lot of coaches wouldn't spend as much time coaching up walk-ons as they do starters, but you do, and that speaks volumes about how much you invest into all of your players.

Running a college football program takes up more time than I can possibly imagine. Despite that, Coach Mark Richt always took time to let every single player know that he cares about them, both on and off the football field. Coach, I really enjoyed the chance to play on your team.

To my college teammates, I appreciate the camaraderie and brotherhood we have. So many of you had an impact on me and gave me pointers that helped me make the team. Specifically, to the linebackers who worked with me as I was trying out, the defensive line group I was part of, the offensive linemen I went against every day in scout team drills, and the walk-ons, I enjoyed going to battle alongside all of you, and I learned a lot from my two years on the team.

To my high school coaches, particularly Kevin Horne and Gerry Romberg, thank you for investing your time in me. What I learned from you in high school football helped prepare me for college.

To my girlfriend, Lauren Pomerantz, thank you for being there for me and helping with decisions related to the content and cover. You were a great sounding board during this process, and this book is better because of it. Brodie was also very helpful.

This book wouldn't have been published without the editing, cover design, and marketing teams that helped me greatly. Natalie, Gail, Erin, Cindy, and Zach, I owe all of you a big thank-you.

ABOUT THE AUTHOR

CANDLER COOK grew up watching University of Georgia football games with his family and decided at a young age that he wanted to be one of those guys on the field. Fourteen years later, he became one when, after his third tryout, he was selected as a walk-on. Candler holds two degrees from the University of Georgia: a bachelor of management and a master of business administration. He lives in Atlanta, Georgia, and works as a finance professional.